LOST RAILWAY JOURNEYS

FROM AROUND THE WORLD

Brimming with creative inspiration, how-to projects and useful information to enrich your everyday life, Quarto Knows is a favourite destination for those pursuing their interests and passions. Visit our site and dig deeper with our books into your area of interest: Quarto Creates, Quarto Cooks, Quarto Homes, Quarto Lives, Quarto Drives, Quarto Explores, Quarto Gifts, or Quarto Kids.

First published in 2018 by White Lion Publishing
an imprint of The Quarto Group
The Old Brewery, 6 Blundell Street
London N7 9BH
United Kingdom

www.QuartoKnows.com

A catalogue record for this book is available from the British Library.

ISBN 978-1-78131-747-1
Ebook ISBN 978-1-78131-853-9

10 9 8 7 6 5 4 3 2 1
2022 2021 2020 2019 2018

Edited by Nick Freeth
Designed by Paul Turner and Sue Pressley,
  Stonecastle Graphics
Maps by Martin Brown

Printed in China

ACKNOWLEDGEMENTS

My grateful thanks to Mike Arlett, Michael Bunn, Keith Chester, Michael Dunn, John Fuller, John Knowles, Peter Lemmey, Nick Lera, Charlie Lewis, Alfred Luft, Julian Peters, Patrick Ridley-Martin, Werner Schleritzko, Mike Schumann, Ted Talbot, Dr Paul Waters, Michael Whitehouse and Donald Wilson who have helped with the loan of books or provided photographs, information and suggestions. Many thanks, too, to the staff of the British Library and the London Library, to Paul Turner and Sue Pressley of Stonecastle Graphics for their patience and the design and to Charlotte Frost for her sound editorial contributions.

LOST
RAILWAY
JOURNEYS

FROM AROUND
THE WORLD

WHITE
LION
PUBLISHING

CONTENTS

Opposite: National Railways of Zimbabwe 15A 4-6-4+4-6-4
Garratt, built by Franco-Belge in 1952, near Wankie.

INTRODUCTION

ANYONE REMOTELY INTERESTED in railways will have read of a remarkable line, or gazed along a trackbed winding through an idyllic landscape, and wished that they could still take a train over it. Numerous books have been published of railway walks down closed lines, and strolling along one it is impossible not to wonder about the men who built and operated them, about the countless people who travelled over them, the reasons for their journeys, the conversations between strangers, the emotions of meetings and partings on now overgrown platforms. Closed railways, as Rose Macaulay said of ruins, invite 'self-projection in the past'.

The 33 journeys in this book have been chosen for their fascinating history, outstanding engineering, the enthralling sights and sounds they once offered, and the landscapes through which they passed – and often for a combination of all four. They wouldn't all be part of any pantheon of great railway journeys had they survived, though many traversed spectacular landscapes. No one could pretend that the original Ghan in Australia wouldn't have taxed the endurance of even the most ardent railway buff. An early passenger wrote: 'Hour after hour, the train jogs steadily along over plains as stony as a badly mended country road. Not a blade of grass is to be seen. The vegetation consists of salt-bush and other salsolaceous bushes, with scrub and perhaps a line of gum-trees marking the course of a distant creek, the shingly bed of which is usually dry.' Hardly copy for a travel brochure.

Opposite: H class 0-4-2 Fell tank No. 201, built by Avonside, began work in 1878. Unsurprisingly conditions in tunnels made the line New Zealand's least attractive for footplate crews.

Yet the story of the railway to Alice Springs is typical of the way railway engineers had to overcome the physical challenges of the terrain, which affected both what they built and how they built it. The challenge of keeping huge workforces fed and watered in inhospitable climates was itself a logistical nightmare on many projects, never mind how stone and iron for structures would be delivered to where they were needed. The indomitable spirit that overcame these obstacles seemed to be passed on to those who came after and ran the railway. Railwaymen – and until recently they were all men – the world over took pride in keeping services running when the elements were against them.

For well over a century the railway was the lifeline of communities and commerce, the railway station a focal point of local life. What was written of a Yorkshire village station could stand for rural stations the world over, details aside: 'The waiting room was quite a social centre. As people gathered to await the arrival of the train they would meet friends and enquire about the anticipated journey...the newsagent could be there, also the local fishmonger and the other tradesmen waiting to collect their wares from the train. In the event of a breakdown or bad weather, arrangements would be made by the stationmaster for a good fire to be burning and...the wife of the stationmaster would bring hot tea for the delayed passengers...the skill and devotion of the staff gained the station garden many first and second prizes for the best kept station on the line.'

Railway travel is sociable and inclusive, helping to create and cement human relations in ways impossible in the alien and insular world of the motor car or lorry. The severing of those bonds within the railway community, and between it and the public, has been regretted in

numerous books and articles. Libby Purves wrote that 'any railway, working properly, is a marvel of civilised co-operation,' and as that poet of industrial-age transport, L.T.C. Rolt, put it, 'a great railway system is perhaps the most elaborate and delicate, yet at the same time one of the most successful, feats of organization ever evolved by man.'

The loss of the railway was much more than a transport inconvenience to countless communities, more than the destruction of something that brought people together. When one looks at the quality of stonework in a bridge abutment, its supported span long gone, it can only be seen as an appalling waste. The railway builders of the nineteenth century generally over-engineered structures to err on the side of caution, given the absence of sophisticated stress calculations that today allow greater precision. Consequently their bridges and viaducts can still carry trains at speeds unimagined by their builders.

During the decades when railways were seen by too many governments as part of the past rather than the future, hundreds of thousands of miles of still valuable and serviceable railway were abandoned with little

thought to the needs of future generations or the welfare of the planet. But there is a darker side to the closures than lack of foresight.

In many countries there is overwhelming evidence that politicians, civil servants and even railway officials deliberately took decisions that would undermine the economic and social case for maintaining a line. Talking to railwaymen in Britain during the 1960s and 70s, it was rare to find one without detailed knowledge of unnecessary expenditure or Machiavellian ways in which passenger and freight traffic had been reduced in order to support the case for closure. That determination was carried through into the indecent haste with which bridges were blown up or removed to block any attempt at reopening. Some of those responsible stood to gain personally from railway closures through their financial interests in road building or haulage.

This skulduggery would be quite reprehensible enough, but the consequences of those closures are little short of criminal. Railway travel is statistically much safer than road journeys: in many countries not a single passenger dies on a railway for years on end, while thousands are killed on the roads every year.

Opposite: A Commonwealth Railways NM class 4-8-0 at Alice Springs in 1937. The class was synonymous with the line until the mid-1950s.

Right: Caledonian Railway 4-2-2 No. 123 runs on to the turntable at Callander before working back to Glasgow with an excursion on 10 October 1964.

By increasing road traffic at the expense of rail, those decision-makers have been responsible for the deaths of countless numbers, at great economic cost, let alone the personal aspects. The scale is huge: globally, 1.25 million died on the roads in 2013, and it is estimated that during the twentieth century 60 million people died in road crashes, about the same number as in the Second World War. These numbers take no account of those who died prematurely through traffic pollution, or the millions disabled or seriously injured in crashes.

The reopening of railways across the world is proof enough that the closures went too far and were ill-considered. Greater environmental awareness, partly through court cases against governments that fail to take meaningful action to reduce traffic pollution, has translated into rising passenger numbers in many countries, with correspondingly fewer young car owners and drivers.

So Sir John Betjeman's prediction, made in 1963, has been proved correct: 'Railways are bound to be used again. They are not a thing of the past and it's heartbreaking to see them left to rot, to see the fine men who served them all their lives made uncertain about their futures and their jobs. What's more it's wrong in every way, when we all of us know that road traffic is increasingly hellish on this overcrowded island...'

Few of the railways in this book are remotely candidates for reopening, leaving us free to self-project into the past, whether or not we have even been to the country they are in. But as the writer Ian Jack perceptively observed: 'Importantly, as I realise from my own childhood admiration for the Caledonian Railway's locomotives in their beautiful livery of light blue, we don't need to have witnessed the real thing to feel nostalgic for it. It often helps if we haven't.'

NOTE

Imperial measurements appear first when they are used historically and are appropriate to the country; otherwise, metric is given first. Railway, station and place/country names have been rendered as they were at the time. No attempt has been made to provide contemporary values to monetary figures, or to decimalize historic currencies.

EUROPE

AUSTRIA

SALZKAMMERGUT-LOKALBAHN

AMONG THE HUNDREDS of light railways that have closed across Europe, few extinctions are as regretted as that of the Salzkammergut-Lokalbahn (SKGLB). It ran for 63km (39 miles) through Austria's lake district between Salzburg and Bad Ischl with a branch to Mondsee. It combined an Alpine setting that Emperor Franz Josef called an 'earthly paradise' with the abundant charm of idiosyncratic narrow-gauge railways – a varied fleet of venerable locomotives, track that was hard to distinguish among flower-filled meadows, cordial exchanges at stations between staff and passengers bound by the ties and sensibilities of rural communities.

Opened in stages during the 1890s, the 760mm (2ft 5⅞in) line was one of many built after an 1880 law – comparable with Plan Freycinet in France (see p.23). The lines would be financially supported, economically built and speeds would be moderate. For decades the railway was inseparable from daily life in the Salzkammergut, and the large numbers of tourists made it a profitable concern until the First World War.

Once out of the Salzburg suburbs, the train ambled through meadows, stopping at wayside halts where a red flag denoted waiting passengers, even though trains stopped anyway. The line was long enough to make the junction of St Lorenz a coaling point, often requiring up to 16 wicker baskets of coal. Leaving St Lorenz, the

Opposite: When there was time for a chat at wayside stations. Krauss-built 0-6-2T No. 10 halts at Plomberg with the midday Bad Ischl–Salzburg passenger train on 29 August 1956.

railway skirted the Mondsee, sharing a ledge above the water with a road, before climbing steeply through woodland to a summit tunnel boring the hill that separates the Mondsee from the even more attractive Wolfgangsee. As the train clung to the southern shore, passengers could watch the steam rack locomotives of the Schafbergbahn climbing to the 1,783m (5,850ft) peak and cliff-edge *gasthaus* of 1862 – as they still do. Leaving the lake, the railway paralleled the River Ischl through a string of villages and unstaffed halts where the local inn might be the ticket office. After another tunnel, the line met the standard gauge again at Bad Ischl. Arcane but astonishing is the fact that the SKGLB had 432 level crossings of one kind or another, only three of them guarded.

Such byways were seldom patronized by royalty; narrow-gauge royal saloons were almost unknown, but the Salzkammergut-Lokalbahn had one for Franz Josef, who spent 82 summers in Bad Ischl, most of them at the Imperial Villa (Kaiservilla) which he and his wife Elizabeth, or 'Sisi', were given as a wedding present. Brahms and Johann Strauss II were among the musicians from Vienna who were privileged to use the imperial saloon, which rather went down in the world after the death of Franz Josef in 1916.

The carriage that served as the imperial saloon until 1906 has an unusual story. That year it was replaced by a new carriage, S152, and became a carriage on the Mondsee branch until 1927 when it was converted into a railcar for the branch. That inveterate traveller of European secondary lines, Bryan Morgan, left a

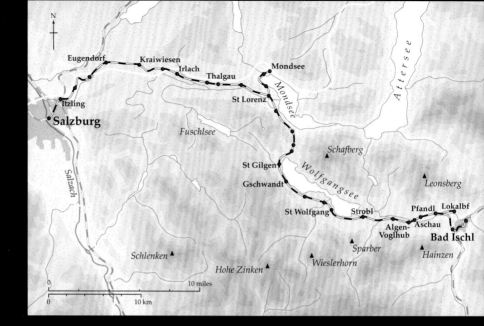

Below: No. 12, the last of the classic 0-6-2Ts delivered to the SKGLB, skirts Lake Wolfgang at Lueg with a Salzburg–Bad Ischl train on 28 July 1957.

description of its eccentricity. He thought it 'built mostly of cardboard, with a minute driving-cab, a small passenger compartment and a large luggage-van which is not used for luggage (this being piled on the buffer-beams) but to house a power unit which consists of the kind of motor one uses for an outboard coupled to the kind of dynamo one uses for lighting a small country house. When the car is in motion this antique device roars and races and leaps about and generally gives the impression that the motors are being fed with some watts well worth having...'

Though not entirely clear from Morgan's description, the engine was very small and the power plant very large, and it was this mismatch which produced sounds like 'a demented mowing machine' in the words of another writer. It was rebuilt various times to improve its efficiency, and it survives today as a bar-car on the Murtalbahn (Tamsweg–Mauterndorf).

There is little doubt that had the SKGLB survived into the 1960s all or part of it would have been saved. Even during the last year of operation, the line carried some 800,000 passengers and 30,000 tons of freight, much of it timber from rail-connected sawmills. But this was a time

when most politicians and planners were myopically convinced that the future lay with the motor car, lorry and bus, oblivious to their harm. As usual, the people affected by the decision were ignored, despite 2,000 of them demonstrating on the streets of Salzburg and 50,000 signing a petition deploring the closure. These days, with the Salzkammergut's roads so busy, local politicians don't hesitate in saying how they wish the railway had survived.

The railway is remembered by a small museum in the single-road engine shed at Mondsee with a model of the branch, photographs, and two of the 0-6-2 tanks from the railway, Nos. S4 and S9. It also contains the first imperial saloon built in 1890 (S1). The 0-6-2 tanks Nos. 5, 11, 12 and 22 (0-6-0), as well as the only diesel, D40, plus several coaches, are sometimes used on the Taurachbahn of Club 760 between Tamsweg and Mauterndorf in the state of Salzburg.

THE ORIENT EXPRESS

THE ORIENT EXPRESS is an anomaly in this book. The journey between Paris and Istanbul can still be made by a succession of shorter service trains, but only once a year is it possible to take a single train between the cities – and one needs a very deep pocket to do so. Belmond's Venice Simplon-Orient Express emulates as closely as possible the route of that first train in 1883 which set the gold standard for luxury railway travel.

No train has captured the imagination of the world like the Orient Express. It has meant many different things to people since its inaugural run: indulgence, escape, romance and sex, a means of making contacts and obtaining information. For most, however, it was simply a convenient and luxurious way to travel across more countries than any other international train. Transcending borders in style and comfort was the purpose of *Compagnie Internationale des Wagon-Lits et des Grands Express Européens*, the firm set up in 1872 by the Orient Express's creator, the Belgian Georges Nagelmackers. CIWL was to dominate international train travel in Europe for much of the next century.

Nagelmackers used his experience of railroad car design in the USA, where he had been sent by his parents to get over rejection of his amorous advances by a cousin, to develop much more luxurious dining- and sleeping-car accommodation in bogie coaches. Most coaches in Europe then had fixed axles and four or six wheels, but bogies provided a more comfortable ride and allowed construction of longer vehicles. After a decade of vicissitudes with shorter routes across the Continent, Nagelmackers finally obtained agreement from all the parties along the line between Paris and Istanbul to inaugurate a service between them.

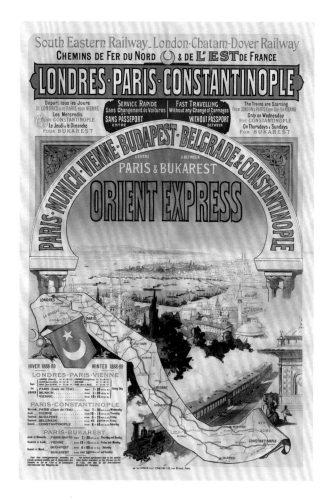

Opposite: A westbound Simplon-Orient Express running beside Lac Léman with Chillon Castle, made famous by Byron, in the background. The train had its origins in the Simplon Express of 1906.

Right: CIWL produced colourful and striking posters for the Orient Express, this one covering the winter service of 1888–89.

On the evening of 4 October 1883 Parisians flocked to Gare de Strasbourg (now Gare de l'Est) to witness the departure of this new train with its invited and fare-paying passengers. The *Express d'Orient* – it became the Orient Express in 1891 – was a revolution in railway travel, with its Westinghouse brake system, heating by low-pressure boiler, and sleeping compartments with washbasin in a corner fitting. But it was the dining-car that astonished the press: it had inlaid marquetry in teak and mahogany panelling, gold-framed etchings and aquatints on the walls, and figures from Greek mythology, created by students of the Paris Art Academy, graced its ceiling. Astride the tables, arranged for two and four diners, were Spanish leather armchairs, with spring-loaded roller blinds and damask curtains covering the windows. A small drawing-room, with Louis XV chairs and a small chaise longue within walls covered by tapestries in the style of Watteau's *fêtes galantes*, was

Below: The brass crest and lettering of CIWL was placed on the dark blue sides of all its coaches.

provided for the exclusive use of female passengers. At the other end of the restaurant car was a gentlemen's smoking room with a small library of travel guides and newspapers in English, French and German.

At the principal cities, the train entered stations *en fête* with reception parties, bands and curious onlookers. Within a fortnight of that successful first run, a King's Messenger was using the service, in a foretaste of the train's role as a conduit for official and unofficial international business. It took a few more years for the train to hit the headlines for all the wrong reasons. A number of journalists on the inaugural train had taken the precaution of carrying revolvers because of the lawless nature of the Balkans, and in 1891 their fears were realized when the train was derailed by Greek bandits. The three CIWL carriages remained on the rails after the coupling between them and the leading carriages broke, but the locomotive and non-CIWL carriages behind it were not so lucky, rolling down an

embankment moments after the driver and fireman had jumped for their lives.

The leader insisted they were freedom fighters, not bandits, and even returned objects of great personal value such as wedding rings in exchange for tobacco. Five of the chosen hostages taken off into the forest were German, and a serious diplomatic incident with Turkey was narrowly avoided when the hostages were returned unharmed after the Ottoman government had paid for their release. Though the crime was hardly welcome publicity for Nagelmackers, millions of Europeans, unaware until then of the still relatively young train, certainly knew about it after so many days of sensational news that enhanced the mystique surrounding it.

Its status was reinforced by the people who used it. Most of the early and first-class passengers would have featured in national or international *Who's Who*. The French diplomat and author Paul Morand described the passengers before 1914 as 'a microcosm of our world', one that included Austrian aristocrats, 'each owning a score of castles and a hundred villages', English milords, Hungarian counts, Romanian boyars, American businessmen in search of Middle Eastern oil concessions,

Below: An Austrian Southern Railway compound 2-8-0 designed by Karl Gölsdorf at Salzburg station with the Orient Express.

the occasional maharaja. After the First World War, those who survived the overturning of the old order were diluted with Greek shipowners, stockbrokers, stars of the stage and screen, impresarios and spies – generally identified with ease by regular travellers. Between the wars, many wealthy Americans joined the British aristocracy in spending part of the year on the French and Italian rivieras.

Among the famous names associated with the train were the exotic dancers Mata Hari and Josephine Baker, Robert Baden-Powell, Calouste Gulbenkian and the arms dealer Basil Zaharoff, as well as a host of royals. Leopold II of Belgium used it to meet his current mistresses while he travelled the Continent making his rapacious business deals to exploit the Congo as his personal fiefdom. The popular Austrian Empress Elisabeth, known as 'Sisi', used the train regularly during her strained marriage to the cold-hearted Franz Joseph, before she was assassinated in Geneva in 1898. Both Ferdinand I and his son Boris III of Bulgaria insisted on driving the locomotive as the train passed through their country. The future George VI took the Orient Express when attending a royal marriage in Belgrade in 1922, but the most frequent British royal

Above: Hungarian Railways (MAV) 424 Class 4-8-0 steam locomotive No 424.010 about to leave Budapest East station with the Simplon-Orient Express in 1929.

Opposite: The bar car of Belmond's Venice Simplon-Orient Express which upholds the traditions of Nagelmackers' great train.

user was Edward VIII, who, when Prince of Wales, used the pretext of attending ear clinics in Vienna to visit its night clubs, before his association with Mrs Simpson. He continued to use the train after his abdication.

As airline competition increased after the Second World War, use of the Orient Express declined, as did the quality of the train. Various threats to discontinue it came and went, but from 20 May 1977 Istanbul ceased to be its destination, as the last train left Paris Gare de Lyon – 13 minutes late so on the 20th instead of the 19th – for its original terminus. The service was cut back to Vienna, though the now geographically incorrect name was retained. The last amputation in the train's lingering death came on 8 June 2007 when the Orient Express left Gare de l'Est for the last time after 124 years.

GEORGES LAMBERT CASIMIR NAGELMACKERS

Georges Nagelmackers was born on 24 June 1845 in Liège in the new state of Belgium, established in 1832. Both his parents were well connected: his father had inherited a family banking firm which had financed trade and industry since the Middle Ages; his mother was a member of one of the country's foremost families, the Frère-Orbans. Their social links extended to the country's royal family, and included its first monarch, Leopold I, uncle to Queen Victoria. Nagelmackers built up a company running over 1,000 railway cars, not only in Europe but across Asia and North Africa, and operating hotels that included the famous Pera Palace in Istanbul and the Grand Hôtel des Wagons-Lits in Peking. The Orient Express's creator died of a heart attack on 10 July 1905 at his château in Villepreux-les-Clayes, situated in the department of Yvelines on the railway between St-Cyr and Dreux.

The opening of the high-speed *Train à Grande Vitesse* (TGV) line between Paris and Baudrecourt reduced the journey time between the French capital and Strasbourg by 100 minutes, so the stump of the Orient Express between Strasbourg and Vienna was timed to provide a connection with a TGV arrival from Paris. At Karlsruhe it was attached to an overnight train from Amsterdam to Vienna. This sorry reminder of the world's best-known train was finally put out of its misery on 12 December 2009, when EuroNight train number 469 Orient Express left Strasbourg for the final time and the famous name disappeared from scheduled timetables after 126 years.

NICE–COLOMARS–GRASSE–DRAGUIGNAN–MEYRARGUES

A GREAT IMPETUS was given to railway construction in France by the Freycinet Plan of 1878–9, which identified 181 new lines to stimulate economic development and to provide many more citizens with access to a railway. The plan was named after its architect, Charles de Freycinet, who became Prime Minister on four occasions following a career with the Chemins de Fer du Midi, latterly as its traffic manager. To reduce costs, many lines were built as roadside tramways to metre gauge (3ft 3⅜in) and classified as railways of *Intérêt Local*. No less than 11,318km (7,074 miles) were added to the railway network in the heyday of such lines during the 14 years before the outbreak of the First World War.

They became the most characterful of railways, linking villages and market towns and winding through bucolic countryside, their few daily trains barely disturbing the peace of *La France profonde*. They coincided with the great age of the postcard, and the stalls of flea markets in French towns and cities once offered choice pickings for those who collected cards of long-abandoned rural byways. Today these railways are remembered in dozens of astonishingly detailed books illustrated by those postcards.

Of the lines built soon after the Freycinet Plan was approved, one of the most interesting was what became the Chemin de Fer de Provence 'main line'. It left the still-open Nice–Digne line at Colomars and headed west through the Alpes Maritime and the world capital of perfume at Grasse to Draguignan, ending in a tree-shaded square in Meyrargues, 210km (131 miles) from Nice. It ran beside roads, sliced through forests, and straddled valleys on great arched viaducts that would prove the line's nemesis.

The line opened in stages between 1888 and 1892 and its services soon gained the nickname of *Train des Pignes*, apparently from the women who collected pine cones in the woods and left them in bags beside the line. The trains moved so slowly that it was not difficult to board them and hoist the bags aboard, taking home a supply of fuel for the fire. The explanation is made credible by the fact that in 1913 it took more than 11 hours to travel the 210km (131 miles), giving an average speed of 19km/h (less than 12mph). Nonetheless, the line was far from a light railway in its structures and trains, and was the first narrow-gauge route in France to exceed 100km (62½ miles).

Among the most impressive viaducts was Siagne, a 72m (236ft) high lattice girder structure spanning the river of the same name in a gorge so deep that a funicular was built to convey building materials. There were several multi-arch stone viaducts, most attractively the curved 11-arch Loup Viaduct set against a craggy defile, but perhaps the most remarkable bridge was the 400m (1,312ft) Pont de la Manda across the River Var at Colomars. This truss bridge carried a road within its box and the railway above. In the early years the locomotive fleet included 0-6-0 and 2-4-0 tender engines whose tanks were replenished at elegant fluted water columns.

Opposite: The Loup Viaduct was one of the highlights of the journey, towering over the village in the Alpes-Maritimes.

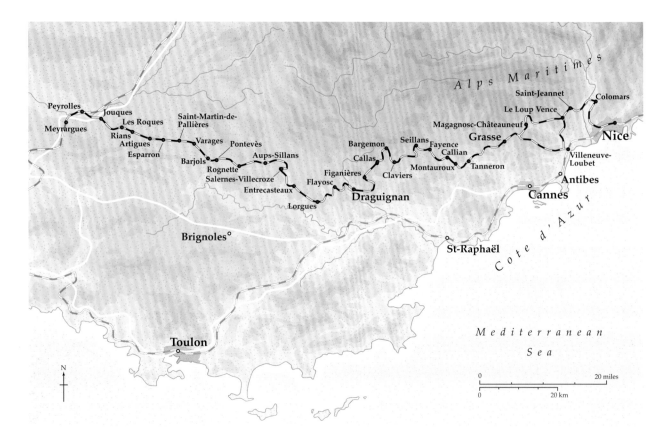

Trains left Nice from the magnificent Neo-classical Gare du Sud, probably the grandest of French metre-gauge stations. Behind its imposing façade of 1890–2 is the rather bizarre train shed designed by Gustave Eiffel, its tall, narrow proportions explained by the structure's reuse from the Paris Universal Exposition of 1889 – where it had been the Russian and Austro-Hungarian pavilion. The station's importance increased with the opening of the line to Digne in 1911. It was replaced by Gare de Nice CP station in 1991, and has since been converted into a library and other cultural facilities.

The slow speeds led to the railway being operated in sections, meeting local needs rather than catering for full journeys. In 1931, surveys looked into converting the railway from metre to standard gauge, but nothing was done. Passenger numbers more than doubled with the acceleration provided by the diesel railcars introduced in 1935, and wartime restrictions on fuel filled more

seats. Responsibility for the destruction of viaducts on 24 August 1944 has been ascribed to Germans during the fighting that followed Operation Dragoon, the Allied invasion of southern France. But some locals, instead of blaming the Germans, believe there was a Machiavellian plan to force the construction of better roads, thereby raising property prices after the war. The likelihood of rebuilding the railway would have been minimal, given that the fortunes of such lines were in doubt even before the war – the route kilometres of *Intérêt Local* lines had fallen from over 20,000 in 1928 to about 12,000 by 1939.

Whoever was responsible, four arches of the Loup Viaduct, two arches of the Pascaressa Viaduct near Tourrettes-sur-Loup and two spans of the Siagne Viaduct were destroyed. Quotes for reconstruction were obtained when peace returned but no work was done, and services were confined to the Meyrargues–Tanneron section. Its hopeless economics prompted the decision to close,

Above: France's metre-gauge railways once had many impressive civil engineering structures, in contrast to many other European countries where costs on narrow-gauge lines were kept to a minimum.

Right: Chemins de fer du Sud de la France (SF) No. 89 was one of 12 4-6-0Ts built by Pinguely in Lyon in 1905–7. Colomars was the junction on the Nice–Digne line where the Meyrargues line turned west.

despite protests from some municipalities, and the last train left Meyrargues station on 2 January 1950.

Much of the trackbed has been turned into roads, its origin betrayed by sweeping curves and stone-walled slopes flanking the tarmac. The equally scenic line between Nice and Digne survived, and has become one of Provence's major tourist attractions as well as a valued link for local communities.

CF DE PETITE CEINTURE

THIS JOURNEY IS an odd one out in the selection. It would not have been much of a delight to the senses, since it would have taken the passenger through some uninteresting parts of France's capital, large sections were in cuttings, and it afforded few sights that draw visitors to the city. But its genesis was exceptional, it contained some impressive structures, and it illustrates the all-too-common failure of city and national governments to anticipate future needs.

The *Chemin de Fer de Petite Ceinture* ('little belt') railway ran just inside the city walls and opened in stages between 1852 and 1867. It was built with the primary purpose of taking troops, ammunition and provisions to the fortifications along the 33km (21-mile) Thiers Wall – named after a prime minister, this had been constructed in 1841–4 with bastions and glacis. Providing connections for freight traffic between the five dominant railway companies which had lines radiating from Paris was secondary, and to begin with no passenger service was anticipated, since the railway ran largely through fields. It took over five years to put the ownership syndicate and finance in place, and some of the sections that eventually formed La Petite Ceinture were not conceived as part of it.

La Petite Ceinture ran mostly above ground except for a long tunnel in the east of the city between Avenue Jean Jaures and a point just north of Charonne station. Railway lines radiating from the city penetrated the walls at eight points, and interchange stations were built at some of the crossing places with La Petite Ceinture:

Orléans-Ceinture station with the CF de Paris à Orléans, and Ouest-Ceinture with the CF de l'État, for example. By the time the last section was finished, Paris had grown rapidly, and the 'country communes' between the inner city tax walls of 1784–91 and the Thiers Wall had been annexed. Transport for these new arrondissements had become a priority, as was completion of La Petite Ceinture before the 1867 International Exposition – which attracted 9.2 million visitors.

The most spectacular structure on the line was the 1,073m (3,520ft) Auteuil Viaduct across the River Seine. Built in 1863–5, it was captured on canvas by various artists including Paul Signac and Maximilien Luce. Long sections were built on arched viaduct reminiscent of the London & Greenwich Railway, with elevated stations such as Point du Jour. Freight trains trundled round La Petite Ceinture between the marshalling yards of the various companies to exchange traffic, operated from 1861 by CF du Nord and later Ceinture Syndicate 0-8-0 tanks. A new slaughterhouse at Vaugirard, opening in 1867 to replace several abattoirs, was linked to La Petite Ceinture at the insistence of Napoleon III.

Only government pressure induced the railway companies to begin passenger services in 1862. A full circuit became possible in 1869, though passengers still had to change trains between companies until 1889. La Petite Ceinture fulfilled its original purpose during the Franco-Prussian War of 1870–1, but the damage caused by Prussian shells during the siege of Paris was eclipsed by the havoc of the subsequent Commune.

La Petite Ceinture was the city's first mass transit line, and passenger frequencies gradually increased to 4–8 trains an hour, requiring a limit on or rescheduling of freight trains. This congestion led to construction of a CF

Opposite: The building of Ménilmontant station on La Petite Ceinture in the 20th arrondissement was typical of France's approach to standardized station structures.

Left: Montrouge station near the Orléans Gate is a protected building in a style typical of la Compagnie des Chemins de fer de l'Ouest.

Opposite: Auteuil Viaduct was a two-storey viaduct of 151 arches linking the town of Auteuil and the Point-du-Jour bridge.

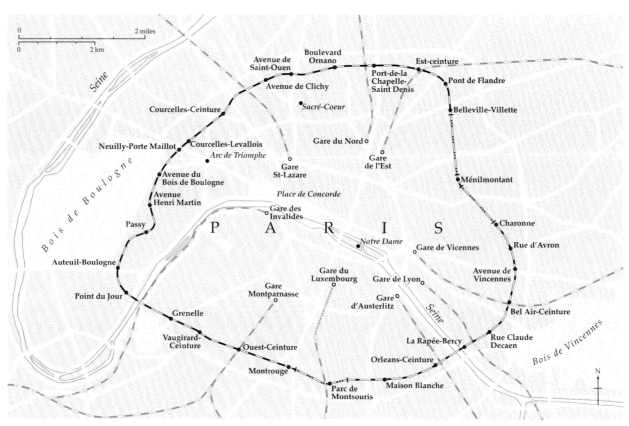

de Grande Ceinture, opening in 1881, to allow the inner ring to concentrate on passenger traffic between its 29 stations with Courcelles-Ceinture in north-west Paris as the principal station. By the Universal Exposition of 1889, when the Eiffel Tower was inaugurated, it was carrying over 18 million passengers a year in mostly unheated, double-deck second-class carriages with an open top deck. First-class carriages were single deck.

By the 1900 Universal Exposition, the double-deck cars had gone and all stock was electrically lit. Passenger

numbers that year reached almost 40 million, which was to prove a peak: the first Métro line opened in July and began to attract passengers away from La Petite Ceinture's 196 daily services. The often enclosed, white-tiled stations of the electric Métro contrasted with the wind- or rain-swept stations and steam-worked trains of La Petite Ceinture. By 1911 numbers were down to 17 million, prompting a further reduction in frequencies. Made obsolete by the changed nature of warfare, the Thiers Wall was demolished from 1919 and its foundations were later used to construct the Boulevard Périphérique.

By 1930 just 4.1 million passengers used the line, and talks began about ending the service. The last regular passenger train on La Petite Ceinture ran in July 1934, replaced by the PC bus line and leaving the tracks again free for more profitable freight (in 1948 an average of 105 freights a day ran on the line). It continued to be used by the service gathering mail for Britain from the Paris termini, and between Nord and Lyon stations by boat trains serving London and Switzerland, the Riviera and central Europe. Closure of the orbital passenger service marked a failure of planning, since no large-scale urban development projects had been created around the stations, but even 21st-century planners in cities choked with congestion and pollution still fail to exploit the potential of mass-transit nodes.

The goods service began to decline from the 1970s, coming to an end in 1993. The Auteuil Viaduct was demolished in 1962, and part of the route was taken over by Line C of the RER (Réseau Express Régional) which opened in 1979. Debate continues over the best use of the rest of the line, but it is at least protected to keep options open. Ironically, Paris is building an orbital tram route (T1–3) and there was talk of using La Petite Ceinture for it, but the Boulevards des Maréchaux ring road around the eastern side of Paris was chosen instead.

In the meantime La Petite Ceinture has become a haven for wildlife with 220 species of plants and animals. A few sections have been opened for walkers: in the 16th arrondissement between Porte d'Auteuil and Gare de la Muette; and in the 15th arrondissement a 1.5km (1-mile) section between Place Balard and Rue Olivier de Serres where the entrance is at 99 Rue Olivier de Serres. Ornano station at Porte de Cligancourt has become a café/ restaurant and urban farm.

PAU–CANFRANC–TARDIENTA VIA SOMPORT TUNNEL

SOME OF EUROPE'S finest railways thread the Pyrenees, and the one with the longest tunnel through the mountains was built partly to shorten the distance between Toulouse and Barcelona. The line between Pau and Tardienta and Zaragoza was built in stages between 1883 and 1928, and it would still be open had a train not run away in 1970 and damaged the L'Estanguet bridge south of Accous so seriously that the central section between Bedous and Canfranc was closed 'temporarily'. It has never reopened.

It was the Chemin de fer du Midi which built the line through the Gave d'Aspe valley as far as Bedous over undemanding terrain. From Bedous the line began the climb into the Pyrenees, first at 1 in 40 and then at 1 in 23. The line wound along mountain sides with 14 tunnels, including a spiral tunnel beyond Urdos at Forges d'Abel, just before the Somport Tunnel and the summit of the line at 1,211m (3,973ft) above sea level. The ascent to the tunnel on both sides was described by one traveller as 'indescribably grand'.

An international convention between France and Spain was required to establish the arrangements for the summit tunnel and interchange between the different track gauges at Canfranc on the Spanish side of the tunnel. Work started in 1912 on the 7.875km (almost 5-mile) dead straight single-track tunnel, but there is

some confusion over its completion date; however, according to the *Railway Magazine* the first public train ran through the tunnel on 20 May 1928. Both stone portals were elaborate, with square towers flanking false machicolations above a heraldic shield. The full opening was officiated by King Alfonso XIII of Spain and French President Doumergue on 18 July 1928.

Canfranc's immense three-storey station building is 241m (791ft) long and dates from 1921–5. Appropriately, its architect, Fernando Ramírez de Dampierre, held dual French/Spanish nationality and had studied in Paris; hence the hint of Gare d'Orsay about its design. Its huge size seems excessive even for its prime function of handling passengers and freight transiting between the two countries, with associated staff accommodation. The number of French staff based there was sufficient to justify a school for their children. Operationally the station was similar to Cambridge with a long platform and scissors crossover in the middle.

The railway from Canfranc to Zaragoza was operated by the Norte-owned Central Aragon Railway which was expected, according to the *Railway Magazine* in 1933, to send a considerable freight traffic in oranges through the tunnel. The line descends through Jaca to a junction on the Zaragoza–Lleida line at Tardienta, with some gradients as steep as 1 in 25. The French side had been electrified for the opening at 1500V DC, but trains on the Spanish side were worked by small-wheeled 0-6-0 and 0-8-0 tender locomotives.

During the Spanish Civil War the Somport Tunnel was closed and bricked up, but it was reopened and

Opposite: The imposing Spanish portal in Canfranc, Huesca. The tunnel's opening shortened the distance between Toulouse and Barcelona by 110km (69 miles).

continued in use during the Second World War when the principal traffic was tungsten north and grain south. The tunnel was also the route for gold payments for the tungsten, and it was used by the Surrealist painter Max Ernst to escape German-occupied France, with the help of Peggy Guggenheim whom he married when they reached the US in 1941.

After the Second World War, the railway functioned as a secondary line, mostly for freight. It was a southbound nine-wagon load of grain on 20 March 1970 that brought an end to its services. An electrical substation was out of order, reducing the power available to the two locomotives as they climbed towards the tunnel. They lost traction on the icy rails, and despite the crew's efforts, including throwing ballast under the wheels, the train descended the gradient and ran away out of control, almost destroying the bridge at L'Estanguet, north of Lescun Cette-Eygun station.

Ten years after the runaway disaster, the line on the French side was closed south of Oloron-Sainte-Marie, but worsening road traffic congestion encouraged reopening of the line as far as Bedous after reconstruction and improvement work in 2016.

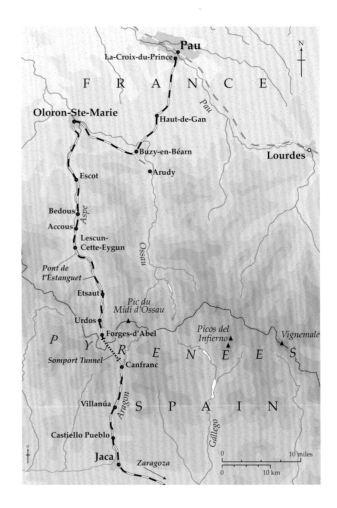

Left: The climb on both sides of the tunnel entailed numerous tunnels, bridges and viaducts. Viaduc d'Escot, completed in 1909, crosses the Gave d'Aspe river.

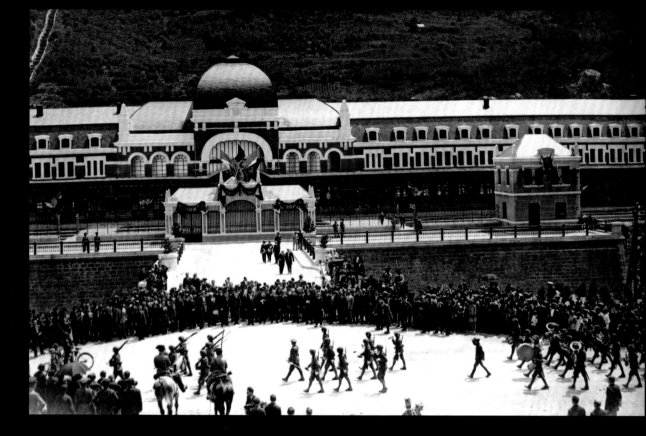

Above: The line was formally opened on 18 July 1928, in the presence of King Alfonso XIII of Spain and the French president, Gaston Doumergue.

Right: The ceremony on 12 July 1912 to mark the start of work on the Somport Tunnel, on which work was delayed by the First World War.

In 2000 the Aquitaine regional council published a report into the reopening of the line for 20-ton axle-load freights and passenger trains, with an eye on tourists in particular. Various options between €50–330 million were examined, and that March the Aquitaine region allocated Fr310 million to the reopening. In 2003, the year the Somport road tunnel opened and exacerbated traffic pollution, Spain funded a study into reopening the rail tunnel, regauging the line from Canfranc–Zaragoza to standard gauge and electrifying it at 25kV. The tunnel has been used as an emergency lane for the road Somport Tunnel, and the Canfranc Underground Laboratory would have to be evicted before work could begin.

Today Canfranc station is regarded as such as extraordinary sight that tours of it are run by the local tourist office, and two trains a day operate from Zaragoza-Delicias station to Canfranc. The roof has been repaired and local authorities have plans to adapt the station building for other uses, including a hotel. Many articles state the station was used as a set in David Lean's 1965 film *Dr Zhivago*, but this appears to be a myth, even though most of the film was shot in Spain.

Below: The dramatic landscape on the Spanish side of the tunnel can be appreciated in this view of Canfranc station.

Left: The ticket window at Canfranc. The station's scale was determined by border formalities for passengers, baggage and freight as well.

Below: The colossal station has 365 windows and was referred to in its early years as the 'Titanic of the Mountains'.

SARAJEVO–BELGRADE

OF ALL THE MANY European narrow-gauge railways, the network of 2ft 6in gauge (760mm) lines in Yugoslavia is especially esteemed – and a route spoken of with particular reverence is the one that wound its way through the mountains between Belgrade and Sarajevo. It was 444km (277½ miles) long, and formed part of a much larger network with another spectacular line through Mostar to the Dalmatian coast at Dubrovnik. The only part of the Sarajevo–Belgrade line built before the First World War was in Bosnia-Herzegovina, which had been occupied by Austria-Hungary in 1878. Though the railway – completed after the formation of Yugoslavia – had its roots in the expediencies of war and politics rather than as a rationally planned contribution to infrastructure, it illustrated that a narrow-gauge system could meet the needs of a sparsely populated, poor region that had challenging terrain. It was a vital part of the economy in Bosnia-Herzegovina and Yugoslavia for a century.

The first section to be built was the Ostbahn from Sarajevo to Vardište. Here, there was a garrison but little else to warrant a railway, though it was already hoped that the line would be extended to join the Serbian narrow gauge. Construction began in 1902, and required a workforce of up to 30,000 men: just supplying their basic provisions – let alone arranging for the delivery of ironwork for structures – was a daunting logistical challenge. The Ostbahn's route from Sarajevo curved round the historic city, affording fine views as it climbed out of the valley along the slopes of Mt. Trebević. The

Karolinen Pass in the Jahorina Mountains was crossed by a long summit tunnel at 946m (3,103ft) above sea level, the highest point on a railway in Bosnia. The line then took the Drina Valley to Višegrad, followed by the Rzava River gorge. Reflecting the railway's strategic purpose, stations were fortified with loopholed steel shutters and walls, and vulnerable structures were protected by watch-towers.

It required 118 bridges and viaducts and 99 tunnels and galleries, and was soon dubbed the 'Bosnian Semmering Railway', a reference to the Austrian line that is now one of three railway World Heritage Sites. Also described by a 1920s visitor as 'uncommonly beautiful', the 166.5km (105 miles) route (including a branch to Uvac) opened in 1906. Soon tourists were using the line. An early book on the Balkans written by Maude Holbach in collaboration with her photographer husband included an account of a journey in 1908: 'What a railway is this that pierces the heart of the wild Balkan mountains! At one moment you are plunged into the darkness of one of the countless tunnels, the next you are enchanted by the beauty of some pastoral scene forming a background for a picturesque group of peasants; then again you find yourself hanging on the edge of a precipice with a mountain torrent thundering below and the cliffs rising in fantastic forms high above you.'

Residents of Bosnia saw it in a rather different light. They, not Austro-Hungarians, shouldered the financial burden of the loans taken out to construct it, and a high proportion of the modest number of passengers were soldiers. Moreover, it had been badly built and required further expenditure to allow heavier locomotives and reasonable speeds. During the First World War the railway was the scene of fighting between Austro-

Opposite: Rack 0-6+4s Nos 97-006 and 97-032 drift down the grade over the Luka gorge viaduct on 9 August 1959.

Hungarian and combined Serbian and Montenegrin forces, which damaged stations and destroyed a few bridges. The major casualty was the bridge over the Drina at Međeđa, but this was rebuilt within eight months.

After the war a conference in Belgrade to plan the transport requirements of the new state of Yugoslavia decided that work should start immediately on extending the railway from Vardište to Užice. Complementing this was the revival of an old scheme for a railway between Belgrade and Čačak, coupled with a link from there to Užice, thereby completing a narrow-gauge main line between the capital and Sarajevo. Recognition of the difficulty the engineers would face in conquering the Šargan mountain between Vardište and Užice was given by splitting the section between two contractors. Work began in March 1921, and three cableways had to be built to carry materials to work sites.

Despite having to bore 20 tunnels between Mokra Gora and Šargan-Vitase stations – the summit tunnel alone was 1,666m (5,466ft) – the line opened in February 1925. The use of a rack was avoided and an average gradient of 1 in 55 achieved by horseshoe curves and

Above: A trolley of what appear to be tourists rather than railway officials crosses the Ostbahn bridge at Dobrik, west of Pale. The remote location of many bridges made them easy wartime targets.

ingenious spirals in a figure-of-eight that form one of the most extraordinary sections of railway in the world, where three levels of track can be seen in a small area, like a fanciful model railway.

The line north of Čačak to Belgrade was opened in stages with final completion in October 1928, marking the formation of a coherent narrow-gauge network rather than a group of unconnected lines, and providing central and southern Yugoslavia with a route to the sea. It was not an easy line to work, with trains spending half the distance squealing around curves, and pilot or banking locomotives being required in places.

The largest class of locomotive was the Class 83 two-cylinder 0-8-2s, the earliest of which were compounded. Between 1903 and 1949, 185 were built by factories in Austria, Hungary, Germany and Yugoslavia. These were supplemented by Class 85 2-8-2s, some built in Hungary as war reparations, and later by a new multi-purpose factory within Yugoslavia at Slavonski Brod.

During the Second World War the line was cut for three months and frequently hit by acts of sabotage and attacks on trains by Tito's Partisan army, which held and operated various sections during its fluid campaign. Whenever they had to move their headquarters in the face

Above: Class 83-034 0-8-2 emerges from one of the Mokra Gora section tunnels on 2 July 1972. The railway resembles a fantasy model with three levels of track visible from mountain viewpoints.

of overwhelming German forces, the Partisans targeted locomotives, rolling stock and bridges. In 1944 the Drina River bridge at Međeđa was again destroyed. Over half the country's railways were damaged or wiped out by the war, but trains were running again between Sarajevo and Belgrade by the end of 1945, in time to help deliver winter supplies of Bosnian coal to Belgrade and Serbia.

Though the railways were restored, the combination of new roads and standard-gauge railways gradually eroded the importance and traffic of the narrow gauge. Some lines could be regauged, but that was out of the question with most of the Sarajevo–Belgrade line. In its final years, before through services between the two cities ended in 1968–9, trains took just over 14 hours, the last departure leaving Belgrade at 17.25 and arriving

Above: A Class 85 2-8-2, probably No. 85-015, framed by unlined tunnels between Međeđa and Ustiprača. As the spectacular terrain indicates, the line could have become a major tourist attraction.

Below: Class 85-015 2-8-2 crossing monumental embankment works near Ustiprača in June 1967 on a westbound train.

in Sarajevo in time for breakfast at 07.30. It was one of very few narrow-gauge railways on which trains ran with sleeping-cars.

The arrival of 25 diesel locomotives in 1968 and 15 in 1970 suggested a future for the narrow gauge, but construction of standard-gauge railways gradually broke up the cohesiveness of the narrow gauge. Once the cost and inconvenience of a break of gauge abstracted long-distance traffic, the writing was on the wall. Though the line between Titovo Užice and Višegrad closed on 1 March 1974 and the final section on to Sarajevo on 28 May 1978, that was not quite the end of the railway. The track between Mokra Gora and Šargan-Vitase stations had been left in deference to the role of Partisans during the Second World War, but it was lifted in the late 1980s. However, a campaign by Serb railway enthusiasts came to fruition in 2000 with the reopening of the upper section between Jatare and Šargan-Vitase; and three years later trains were restored between Jatare and Mokra Gora, a distance of 14km (8¾ miles). There are plans to reopen the full 43km (27 miles) to Višegrad.

TEBAY – DARLINGTON OVER STAINMORE SUMMIT

THE IMAGE INDELIBLY associated with this trans-Pennine route is a string of iron-ore wagons with locomotive front and rear on the gossamer ironwork of Belah Viaduct. The fields overlooking the viaduct were a favoured place for those photographers happy to wait on a windswept moor for their pictures, which might often be spoilt by wind blowing the smoke over the train or the structure beneath it. Until weight restrictions on the viaducts were eased under British Railways, trains were often hauled by locomotives that were under-powered for the traffic, and double-heading and noisy exertions were called for.

The first part of the network of lines, from the East Coast main line at Darlington to Barnard Castle and on to junctions with the West Coast main line, was opened in 1854, and presented no difficulties to its engineer, Thomas Bouch. The second part would be very different. It was only the expectation of lucrative traffic in coke westbound to the ironworks of west Cumberland and Barrow-in-Furness, and haematite iron ore eastbound from the Ulverston area to the ironworks of Middlesbrough, that encouraged its promoters. Passenger traffic was barely mentioned in the prospectuses of the South Durham & Lancashire Union Railway, a line to link the Stockton & Darlington Railway (SDR) near Bishop Auckland with Tebay. It would form a junction at Barnard

Castle with the line from Darlington, and bifurcate at Kirkby Stephen for Penrith along the Eden Valley and a more southerly line to a junction with the West Coast main line at Tebay. From Barnard Castle a branch headed north-west to the small market town of Middleton-in-Teesdale which once depended on lead mining and stone quarries.

The South Durham & Lancashire Union Railway also chose Bouch as its engineer; he devised a route through the Pennine pass at Stainmore that avoided the need for tunnels but required many viaducts. Work began in 1857, and the lines opened in stages between 1861 and 1863, operated by the SDR which became part of the North Eastern Railway (NER) in 1863.

The steep-sided Pennine river valleys which the trains crossed on a mixture of masonry and steel viaducts made for wonderfully scenic journeys over all the routes. The moorland landscapes were doubtless enjoyed by passengers on the Newcastle–Blackpool trains which were the principal long-distance service. There was even a short-lived boat train between Newcastle and Barrow. Until the 1950s the line was busy night and day with mineral trains raising echoes across the empty hills; by the 1880s a million tons of coke a year were being moved westwards over the line. Sidings along the main line served lime and stone quarries, and there was agricultural traffic of livestock and milk as well as coal and general merchandise.

Barnard Castle was one of the busiest cross-country junctions in the country, with passenger trains in four directions and stone off the Middleton-in-Teesdale

Opposite: BR 3MT 2-6-0 No. 77002 and an unidentified LMS Ivatt 2-6-0 cross Smardale Gill Viaduct with a Blackpool express in the late 1950s. Only one line was ever laid across the structure.

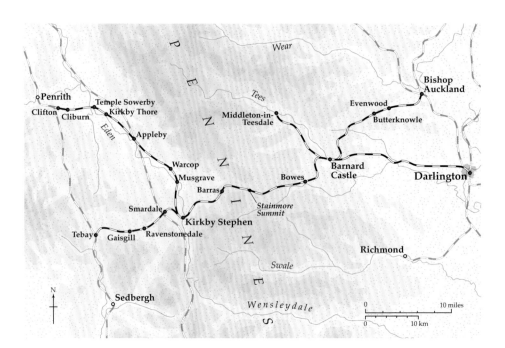

Below: The viaduct across Deepdale Beck under construction, *c.* 1858. Identical in design to Belah Viaduct, Deepdale was 161ft (49m) high and 740ft (225.5m) long.

branch, as well as the trans-Pennine mineral traffic and general freights. The only thing it lacked as a place to watch trains was an engine shed, at least after 1937 when the small affair that had been in use until then was closed. Westbound trains faced a 13-mile (21km) climb that was seldom at less than 1 in 69, calling for pilot or banking locomotives.

Another favoured place to watch trains was the line's highest point, Stainmore Summit at 1,370ft (418m), a bleak spot even in summer, but brutal under a few feet of snow. Longer runs of signal wires had to be on elevated posts to reduce the risk of becoming inoperable, and in the notorious winter of 1947 the snow was so high that gangers could walk over the telephone wires. One of its signalmen recalled that he 'spent the happiest days of my life in this isolated cabin; as an aspiring young signalman I became acquainted with the beauty of a sunrise on a summer morning, the call of the grouse in the heather... or the simple breathtaking majesty of a sunset over the valley. I treasure most of all the memory of the brilliance of the Northern Lights...when it did seem as if the stars could be picked out of their velvet background, so near did they appear.' At the summit there were crossovers for the banking engines and sidings for up and down lines, so the signalman would have plenty of conversation from firemen observing Rule 55, governing the reporting of a locomotive's presence. Guards might also call while fulfilling the requirement to pin down a quarter of the wagon brakes for the descent eastbound, or half westbound.

One of the most celebrated films produced by British Transport Films was made to the west of Stainmore in 1955. *Snowdrift at Bleath Gill* told the story of how a freight between Kirkby Stephen and Barnard Castle, which had become stuck fast and almost buried, was gradually extricated by warming up the moving parts gently to avoid damage. Enginemen working over Stainmore had a reputation as tough characters, especially when working on locomotives with nothing more than a weatherboard or minimal cab to protect them during storms. Exposure to the elements was thought to encourage concentration.

The viaducts were among the finest on any railway in Britain. Most were of masonry, but Belah and Deepdale were built using double Warren truss girders on cast-iron columns to save time in construction. The viaducts at Merrygill, Percy Beck and Podgill are Grade II listed, as is the gloriously situated 14-arch Smardale Gill, which was restored by the Northern Viaduct Trust and is now part of a footpath to a nature reserve.

Belah Viaduct was 1,040ft long (317m), and the highest in England at 196ft (60m). It was in such a lonely position that cottages were built for the signalmen at Belah signal-box at the western end of the viaduct. Though isolated, there were often permanent-way gangers calling in, and

Below: BR Standard 4MT 2-6-0 No 76045 and an LMS Ivatt 2-6-0 cross Belah Viaduct with a train from Blackpool to the North East in the late 1950s. The signal-box can be seen at the far end.

after the Second World War a tramp took up residence in a nearby abandoned cottage and would stop in to regale the signalman with stories of his time in the Army and the Palestine police. For a time after the Second World War a weight restriction was imposed on Belah Viaduct which prevented double-heading, so eastbound trains had to be banked. An admirer wrote that 'seen in a clear moonlight, when the snow is on the ground or a fleecy cloud of mist partly envelops it, and one of the long trains happens to be passing, the whole appears to be more like the work of enchantment than a very solid reality.' And a Victorian poet was moved to extol Belah:

Westmoreland's honour form'd by the skill of man
Shall ever o'er thy spacious landscape span.
And thousands wonder at the glorious sight;
Where trains shall run aloft both day and night...

The first closure came in 1952 with the loss of passenger trains between Kirkby Stephen and Tebay, and all the other passengers and goods services were withdrawn in 1962–5. The case for closure had been put together by means of the deceitful and all too commonly used practice of increasing expenditure on completely unnecessary work to cook the books. Despite the distances that separated them, local communities joined forces to mount a challenge and found numerous inaccuracies in the closure proposals. These even included an inflated figure for replacement of the engine-shed roof at Kirkby Stephen, when steam locomotives were already being phased out. But the Minister of Transport of the day, Ernest Marples – who owned a major road-construction company – approved closure, and the railway was lifted with the usual haste to preclude any possibility of reopening. The magnificent metal viaducts were reduced to scrap, and the Army was invited to practise demolition on the stones of Mousegill Viaduct.

Opposite: BR Standard class 4MT 2-6-0 No 76048 at Kirkby Stephen East with an eastbound passenger train on 25 June 1956. The station was a hive of activity before the line was deliberately run down, and since the 2000s it has become an operating railway heritage centre.

Above: Ivatt 4MT 2-6-0 No 43018 climbs towards Stainmore summit with a westbound coke train banked by a sister engine in spring 1960. The sound of these heavy trains could be heard across the moors night and day for the better part of century.

SIR THOMAS BOUCH

Born in Thursby near Carlisle in 1822, Bouch began his engineering career on the Lancaster & Carlisle Railway and the Stockton & Darlington Railway before going to Scotland to design and introduce the first roll-on/roll-off train ferry service in the world, across the Firth of Forth. He built many railways in Scotland, but he is known primarily for designing the first Tay Bridge. This single-line structure was almost 2 miles (3.2km) long with 86 spans, and opened on 1 June 1878. A year later Queen Victoria travelled over it and knighted Bouch. On the evening of 28 December 1879 a ferocious westerly gale was blowing when a northbound local train of five carriages hauled by North British Railway (NBR) 4-4-0 No. 224 set out from Wormit station and onto the bridge. As it reached the central 'high girders', a fierce gust brought them down and the train disappeared into the water, with the loss of 75 lives. The official inquiry divided blame between Bouch's failure to allow for wind speeds and pressure, and the contractors' slipshod work. Bouch resigned his role with the NBR, his design for a bridge across the Forth was abandoned and he retired to Moffat in rapidly declining health, and died in 1880.

WAVERLEY ROUTE: EDINBURGH–CARLISLE

AMONG THE VARIOUS Scottish lines which should never have been closed, the longest is the 98-mile (157km) main line providing the most direct link between Carlisle and Edinburgh via Hawick, Melrose and Galashiels. There could be no better acknowledgement of the rashness of that decision than the line's reopening, which began in 2015 with the first services over the Borders Railway between Edinburgh and Tweedbank. It is likely to be many years before a train runs further south.

The first part of the line that took the name of Sir Walter Scott's series of novels was assembled in piecemeal fashion, though the company that completed it, the North British Railway (NBR), had long wanted a route to the west coast of England independent of its great rival, the Caledonian Railway. The earliest part of what eventually became a double-track main line even began as a horse-drawn 4ft 6in (1372mm) gauge railway between St Leonards and Dalhousie near Newtongrange. This was converted to standard gauge and used as the start of the line south to Hawick built by the North British Railway and opened in 1849. It was another 13 years before through trains reached the border junction of Carlisle.

The first part to Hawick was expensive to build. From Dalhousie, the line climbed to a summit at Falahill

through the valleys of the South Esk and an 8-mile (12.8km) stretch of 1 in 70. From this pass between the Moorfoot and Lammermuir hills the railway descended the valley of the Gala Water with (initially) 15 timber-built crossings of the stream. After Galashiels, it took the Tweed Valley to reach Melrose, St Boswells and Hawick. The first sod of the second part of the line was turned on 7 September 1859 under a banner that read 'Put a stout heart to a steye brae [steep hill]'. That was certainly demanded of those who toiled through the next three winters in the wildest country of Scotland's lowlands, relying on horses traversing boggy ground to bring in supplies to isolated navvy camps. The terrain didn't stop local people visiting the work to see how 'their railway' was progressing, and a textile mill in Hawick organized a trip to the 1,206yd (1,103m) Whitrope Tunnel works site as its annual outing.

But the first passengers travelling the line in July 1862 saw a landscape dotted with the rusting equipment of failed contractors. It had cost the colossal sum of £5 million, and there were great difficulties recruiting navvies to work in such harsh conditions. Progress was often so slow that one contractor absented himself rather than meet a delegation from the railway company.

The surveyors of both sections of the railway worked their way around natural barriers wherever possible, but there was no alternative to the two fierce climbs to the summits at Falahill and Whitrope, the latter considered a tougher challenge than the Caledonian's Beattock Bank because of the curvature. Leaving the half-way point of Hawick, southbound trains faced 10 miles (16km) of

Opposite: LNER V1 2-6-2T No 67649 after arrival at St Boswells with a train from Kelso. Engine crews chat while station staff load mailbags into the guard's part of the passenger brake coach.

climbing at a maximum gradient of 1 in 70 to Whitrope Summit and the tunnel, and though most drivers declined an assisting pilot locomotive, many accepted a push from one of the veterans based at Hawick shed for lighter duties around the border branches.

Early results from the Waverley route were so disappointing that some directors were even urging abandonment. Only when the Settle & Carlisle railway opened in 1876 did the Waverley route come into its own and start earning more than branch-line revenues. London St Pancras saw expresses leaving for Edinburgh via Carlisle and Hawick, and through freight traffic increased significantly. Besides general merchandise, the principal inbound goods traffic comprised wool for the textile mills of Galashiels and Hawick and coal. Outbound traffic was dominated by livestock and the products of the mills. Stations south of Hawick contributed very little to NBR coffers, but they became well known to railway photographers and sound recordists.

The most eminent of the latter was Peter Handford, who won a BAFTA for the location sound on *Out of Africa*. He said he never found 'any line which offered better recording opportunities than the Waverley route', and he was awarded the *Grand Prix du Disque* in Paris in 1965 for his recording of a V2 class 2-6-2 on a freight near

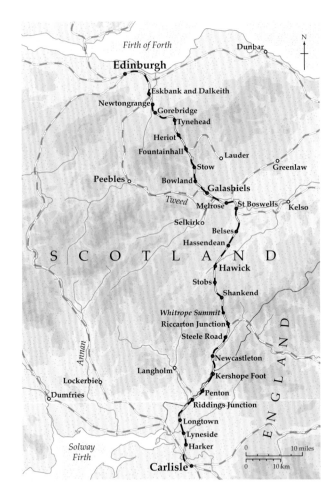

Left: LNER K3 2-6-0 No. 61885 heads an afternoon Carlisle to Edinburgh goods on the 10-mile (16km) climb from Newcastleton to Whitrope summit in 1952.

Above: LNER A3 Pacific No. 60093 Coronach climbs to Falahill summit with a southbound express from Edinburgh Waverley on 15 April 15 1961. Loops and sidings were provided on both sides at the summit.

Steele Road, which was one of the tracks on the Argo Transacord disc 'Trains in the Night'. Steele Road was, in his words, 'a strange, lonely place; the signalbox was only manned as required, and a porter/signalman roamed around the station with a shotgun, looking guilty when anyone approached unexpectedly.'

A lively account of a nocturnal footplate trip on A3 Pacific *Flamingo* described travelling through the dark countryside with occasional lights from isolated houses and farms. There were constant changes in sound from the Gresley locomotive's syncopated exhaust beat and from the train as its passed over and under bridges, headed through cuttings and tunnels, and skirted woodlands. The exhaust reverberated from the surrounding hills that could barely be made out in the dark. The writer noted the glint of the driver's pocket watch taken out to check their timings, the wave of the signalman as they passed Whitrope box, and the way that the crew, even in the dark, could recognize the landmarks that reminded them to look out for signal lamps.

Quite apart from the majestic lowland hills, the journey provided plenty of interest at the various intermediate junctions where branch lines wandered off through equally unpopulated and rugged countryside: Fountainhall Junction for Lauder; the Peebles line trailing in at Kilnknowe Junction north of Galashiels; the Reston and Coldstream branches heading east from St Boswells; the Border Counties line from Hexham at Riccarton; and the Langholm branch at Riddings. How anyone expected them to make a worthwhile (or any) profit is a mystery.

The most extraordinary settlement on the line was Riccarton Junction, a hamlet established in 1862 when it became the junction for the Border Counties line to Hexham. It had no road access until the Forestry Commission created an unmetalled track to it in 1963. Six cottages built by the original contractor were taken over by the railway, and the settlement grew to 33 houses with a population of over 100. An engine shed for six locomotives and a carriage shed were built, and the NBR constructed a gas-manufacturing plant capable of lighting 300 lamps. A refreshment room doubled as Riccarton's only pub, and the Co-op established a shop on the platform – supplied, of course, by train. The sub-post office was a corner of the waiting room.

Initially, church services were sanctioned in the locomotive shed, followed by free-of-charge church trains which ran to Hawick and Newcastleton on alternate Sundays. When these were discontinued, a minister at Saughtree was given a permit to walk the 3 miles (4.8km) along the track. If someone was seriously ill, a locomotive would be dispatched to fetch the nearest available doctor. A small school was built for the younger children, while

the older ones went to Hawick in a carriage attached to the back of a northbound goods. Dances were held in the school hall, and on three evenings a week a late evening train was run for people to visit one of the three cinemas in Hawick.

Harmony did not always prevail at Riccarton. Occasional disturbances required the intervention of the police, and a report on one outbreak revealed that four railway wives were terrorizing the community. The agent sent from Hawick to investigate recommended the transfer of their husbands to different areas of the NBR: 'That will teach their wild venomous women that they cannot be allowed to disturb any community without having to pay some penalty.'

Trains in the early years were in the hands of NBR 0-6-0s and 4-4-0s, often double-headed. To obviate the need for two locomotives, 14 hefty Atlantics arrived from North British Locomotive Co. in Glasgow in 1906 but ran into immediate difficulty. The NBR's civil engineer had not been shown the drawings, and with evidence of broken rails and spread track, he demanded their withdrawal. Moreover, they were too long to fit on to any NBR turntable. Within two years, however, the problems were resolved, and the Atlantics put in good performances over the Waverley route. After the Grouping of 1923 and into British Railways' days, A3 Pacifics handled many expresses with freights in the hands of V2 2-6-2s and K3 2-6-0s, supplemented by the older NBR classes.

The value of the Waverley route lay in the links it provided between urban areas of northern England and Edinburgh; south of Sheffield, trains were lightly loaded. Closure was proposed by the 1963 Beeching Report and formally announced in 1966, but it was under Barbara Castle's 'Network for Development' plans of 1967 that the Waverley route was closed, her successor Richard Marsh signing it off in July 1968 with the assertion that doing so would save £700,000 a year. British Rail had claimed a loss of £232,000, and even the Beeching Report put it

at no more than £113,000. Many realized that no bus or car journey would be an adequate substitute for the train service, and that closure would damage the economic development of a region that needed all the help it could get. Anger at the shutdown among Border residents was so intense that when the last sleeping-car express from Edinburgh reached Newcastleton on 5 January 1969, it encountered probably the most demonstrative protest against a railway closure in Britain. The populace were massed around the level crossing, which was padlocked against the train. In the stand-off, the local minister was arrested, but his release was negotiated by the MP for the area, David Steele – who had fought against closure and was a passenger on the train – and it resumed its journey.

The line closed to passengers on 6 January 1969, and a section of track was symbolically lifted the next day with journalists and photographers in attendance.

SOMERSET & DORSET RAILWAY

OF ALL THE ENGLISH cross-country routes, none has engendered the nostalgia felt for the line that ran up hill and down dale through idyllic countryside in Somerset and Dorset. Those feelings have much to do with the photographs of Ivo Peters, who so brilliantly captured the character and beauty of the line during the nationalized years. Even the station names evoked visions of bucolic summers and rural harmony – Evercreech, Midsomer Norton, Binegar, Wellow – platforms where the peace was broken only by the sounds of agriculture until the 'call attention' bell code in the signal-box heralded a train. It seemed wholly appropriate that such a line, even though most of it closed in 1966, hardly ever heard the blare of diesel horns.

Normally referred to simply as the S&D, the Somerset & Dorset Railway's original purpose was to link the Bristol and English channels by a line between the packet port of Burnham-on-Sea and a junction with the London & South Western Railway at Wimborne. Passenger trains ran on to Bournemouth and goods trains served south-coast towns and ports. Opened in 1863, the line failed to attract the expected traffic, and in a bid to stave off bankruptcy the S&D built a 26-mile (42km) line from Evercreech Junction to Bath and a connection with the Midland Railway. This became the S&D's main line, relegating the Burnham line to branch-line status. But it

was too late to retrieve the financial position; though the northern extension proved the making of the railway by producing a significant increase in traffic, it brought its independent existence to a close, and the line became the joint property of the two companies at each end.

With the Midland and the London & South Western railways taking a 50/50 lease, the railway became the Somerset & Dorset Joint Railway in 1876. The arrangement delighted both companies, since they now had a north-south route independent of the then broad-gauge Great Western Railway. Traffic was quickly developed, with the Midland timetabling through carriages between Birmingham and Bournemouth on two of the four daily trains, but it was summer excursions from many northern and Midland towns and cities that taxed the capacity of the cross-country line. In later years it even had a daily named train, the Pines Express, which linked Manchester and Bournemouth.

Its capital exhausted, an independent S&D would not have been able to take advantage of the new traffic the northern extension generated, but the Joint Committee set about doubling many sections of single line and installing new signalling. The S&D became woven into the life of the community in a way now hard to imagine. The railway served a lime works, a brick and tile factory, and even mines on the Somerset coalfield. Dairy farmers sent their milk to United Dairies at Bailey Gate, and horse-boxes by the dozen went to the races at Wincanton. Cider traffic was a staple at West Pennard, and barrels of Oakhill Invalid Stout were brought to Binegar station by a 2-mile (3.2km) 2ft 6in (762mm) tramway from Oakhill

Opposite: The 7.35am Saturdays only Nottingham to Bournemouth train is about to enter Combe Down Tunnel behind LMS 2P 4-4-0 No. 40696 and S&D 7F 2-8-0 No. 53804. The trackbed is now a cycle route.

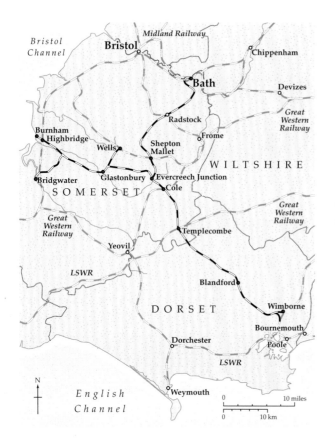

Brewery. Boxes of Lyons cakes would arrive daily from Kensington in London, and Blandford's two fishmongers would meet the first down train at 8.21am to collect fish sent from Hull and Grimsby.

The S&D was a close-knit concern, where staff knew one another up and down the line and generations of a family would be 'on the railway'. It was not unknown for a son to fire a locomotive for his father as driver. Favours transcended distance: plants or a couple of rabbits would often return on the footplate or in the guard's van, the bunnies sometimes dispatched by a 12-bore carried on board, or caught in snares by permanent-way gangers. Many a haircut was done in Chilcompton signal-box, where one of the signalmen was handy with the scissors.

Below: BR's 9F 2-10-0s were a surprising success on the S&D. No. 92212 drifts downhill from Winsor Hill Tunnel near Masbury with the 9.35am Saturdays only Sheffield to Bournemouth train in August 1961.

Above: A daily express inaugurated in 1910 between Manchester and Bournemouth was given the name Pines Express in 1927. The train is here hauled by LMS 2P 4-4-0 No. 40564 and BR Class 5 No. 73050.

Some of the houses for crossing keepers had no running water, so designated freights would carry cans of potable water on the buffer beam, and the keepers would have a weekly pass to do their shopping at the nearest market town. Locomotive crews knew to go slowly on Pylle Bank when hazelnuts were in season so they could lean out from the footplate and pick them, and trains would sometimes reduce their speed to pick up a bag of plums from a farmer. Small wonder the poet John Betjeman chose the Burnham-on-Sea branch as the locale for *Let's Imagine – A Branch Line Railway* (BBC, 1963).

Railway photographers flocked to the line, not only to capture a succession of excursion trains with a pleasing variety of locomotives at the front, but also to savour some of England's finest countryside. The peace would be broken only by the lowing of cattle or rolling of milk churns. Masbury was such a lonely spot that church services were held in the waiting room, accompanied

by a harmonium, and it was among the Saturday evening duties of the porter to prepare the room. The station gardens would generally be someone's pride and joy – that at Midsomer Norton was a mass of flowers, Cole's garden had a fish pond, and the flower-beds at Shillingstone won many awards for 'best-kept station', which may have had something to do with the station's use by Edward VII when visiting Iwerne Minister House. Bowls of primroses would decorate the table of the waiting room at Evercreech.

Besides the array of locomotives that could be seen on summer Saturdays, another attraction for railway buffs was the unique Class 7F 2-8-0 locomotives designed

Left: One of the 11 S&D 7F 2-8-0s, large-boilered No. 53806, climbs to Masbury summit with a coal train from Midsomer Norton in May 1953.

Opposite: The classic country goods yard at Midford is passed by SR Pacific No. 34040 *Crewkerne*, working the 9.05am Bristol to Bournemouth train. The yard's main traffic was Fuller's earth from Tucking Mill.

specifically for the line by Sir Henry Fowler. First introduced in 1914, they never worked anywhere else (other than trials) and performed sterling service until their withdrawal began in 1964.

The steep gradients, often accentuated by the line's curvature, were a further draw for visitors. Though they made it one of the most challenging lines to work in Britain, for the spectator the hills elicited full-throated exhausts from locomotives, and called for banking locomotives from Bath, Radstock and Evercreech. Beyond Bath Junction, where S&D metals began, trains faced a steep climb to Devonshire and Combe Down tunnels, mostly at 1 in 50. The majority of freights had to be banked, the banker dropping off as soon as the brake van was inside Combe Down Tunnel. This was the longest tunnel in Britain without ventilation shafts, making it unpleasant for the crews, especially those on the train engine of a double-headed working. Following a descent at 1 in 100 to Midford, another southbound climb began at Radstock to the summit of the line between Binegar and Masbury at 811ft (247m) above sea level, with long stretches of 1 in 50. The 5 miles (8km) of 1 in 50 down to Evercreech Junction required a banker for northbound

freights and a pilot engine for most passengers.

A trick of banking-engine crews was to fit forbidden 'jimmies' – curved iron hooks that were wedged into the blastpipe to improve the draught and steaming of locomotives. The device was disapproved of because it increased wear by flogging the engine harder. On one occasion, the blacksmith at Radstock engine shed was brought before an inspector, who demanded to know for whom he had made them. The poor man scratched his head and replied that 'it'd be easier to say who I didn't make'n for'.

The S&D's end was a textbook case of closure through dogma, manipulated accounts, official indifference, under-investment – the fastest trains in 1962 were slower than 1913 – and appalling lack of foresight. All but a few freight services over surviving stubs were withdrawn on 7 March 1966.

A 4-mile (6.4km) stretch out of Bath has become part of the popular Two Tunnels Greenway, with LEDs illuminating the resurfaced trackbed in Devonshire and Combe Down tunnels, which forms a 13-mile (20.8km) loop through Midford and back to Bath via the Kennet & Avon Canal towpath.

WARNING.
PERSONS ARE WARNED NOT TO
TRESPASS UPON THE COMPANY'S
RAILWAYS, STATIONS, WORKS, LANDS
AND PROPERTY. ANY PERSON FOUND
TRESPASSING WILL BE PROSECUTED

CALLANDER & OBAN RAILWAY

THE HIGHLAND RAILWAY served one of the most sparsely populated parts of Britain – and yet, of all the railway companies that existed before the Grouping of 1923, is the one that has had the smallest percentage of its lines closed. All its principal routes are still extant, except a section of the old main line across Dava Moor. This reflects the reliance of many rural communities on the railway, especially in winter, and its importance to tourism.

The line through the Highlands that invokes the greatest sense of loss is the Callander & Oban (C&O) between Dunblane and Crianlarich, which became an independent part of the Caledonian Railway rather than the Highland. Opened in stages between 1858 and 1873, its construction was helped by the effects of glaciation in lowering the height of a pass through a watershed and smoothing valley slopes to allow easier gradients along a shelf cut into the hillside.

A measure of its scenic attractions is that the C&O featured in 32 out of 41 tours featured in the Caledonian's 1911 handbook. Three years later, the Caledonian introduced on a daily Glasgow–Oban train a Pullman observation car *Maid of Morven*. It was a unique vehicle, boasting a kitchen, and an observation compartment with 14 moveable armchairs, large side windows and a floor-to-roof bow window at the back. This window almost certainly had the largest pane of glass fitted to any British railway carriage. A lounge area seated eight passengers, and both sections were panelled with finely figured pearwood and separated by marquetry pilasters. Hand-painted silk shades screened the table lamps. Built by Cravens of Sheffield, the coach had to be shunted onto a turntable to place it at the rear of train formations. Its operation was suspended during the war, but reinstated in 1920, and it continued to delight summertime passengers who could afford the 2s 6d supplement until 1937. Bizarrely, the armchairs in the bay window were usually arranged facing inwards, perhaps because it was said that sight of a notable person allowed local gossip to open with a report that 'So-and-so was on the *Maid*'. Pullman restaurant cars operated in Caledonian days and during ownership by the London Midland & Scottish Railway.

The C&O's success in the early years owed much to its general manager, John Anderson. Railways through such empty country called for skilled management and economy, and when the people of Kingshouse between Strathyre and Lochearnhead asked for a station, Anderson told them they could build one themselves – so they did.

The gradients along the line called for strenuous work from the firemen, with climbs as steep as 1 in 47, and a 5½-mile (8.8km) stretch of 1 in 60. Heading west from the junction with the Edinburgh–Perth main line, the first section was double-track to Doune where the fireman collected the single-line tablet for Drumvaich Crossing. This was one of those lonely crossing places found on single lines where a long section between

Opposite: BR Standard Class 4MT 2-6-4T No. 80028 arrives at Killin Junction with the branch train from Killin in July 1965. There was no road access to the interchange station and its three platforms.

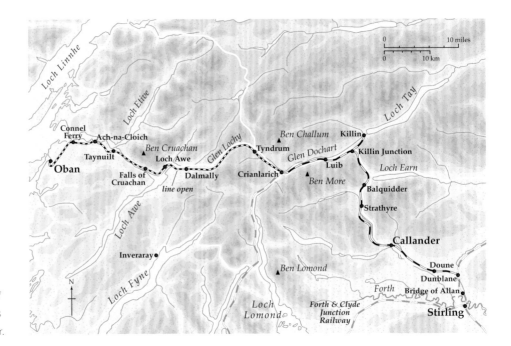

Below: Boat trips have been part of the tourist attraction of Scotland's west-coast ports, as advertised in this c.1901 poster.

stations required a passing loop. Usually accommodation was provided for the signalmen and their families, who would rely on a special stop by a designated train to take children to school and wives to the nearest source of groceries.

Callander station was a large, handsome building with three gables extending into the station forecourt; its wooden construction and steeply pitched roof gave it a slightly Swiss air. The covered footbridge between platforms had the unusual feature of a clock built into its roof, but the whole structure was demolished by a runaway goods train in 1947. The station featured in the BBC's series *Dr Finlay's Casebook* which used Callander for filming the fictional town of Tannochbrae. The dramatic scenery began as the train steamed west from Callander to reach the Pass of Leny and another passing loop at St Bride's Crossing. Passengers in the know would be sitting on the right-hand side of the train for the run beside Loch Lubnaig, enjoying the views of range after range of mountains receding on a bright summer's day into a hazy blue-grey distance.

Permanent-way gangs had particular problems along Loch Lubnaig. One day a ganger was working in the

Above: LMS Class 4-6-0 No. 45358 and a BR Standard Class 5MT 4-6-0 climb away from Killin Junction with an Oban to Glasgow Buchanan Street train on 14 April 1961. The signal-box can be seen on the left.

vicinity when the telegraph wires above him suddenly jerked and the sound of falling rock came from around the bend. The line was completely covered in rocks so large that the heaviest crane could not lift them, and they had to be blasted into manageable sizes. This was one of several places on the C&O prone to rock avalanches, and taut wires linked to signals were placed to detect rock falls. Devised by Anderson, the wires emitted a musical hum during winds, and older railwaymen referred to them as 'Anderson's piano'.

At the head of the loch was the station serving the village of Strathyre where William Wordsworth stayed in 1803 and was inspired to write 'The Solitary Reaper'. Soon after Kingshouse station, the train rolled into Balquhidder, once a delightful country junction with two signal-boxes where a branch line turned eastwards to skirt Loch Earn on its way to Crieff and Perth. The climb continued through rock cuttings and over impressive embankments for another 6 miles (9.6km) to Glenoglehead and magnificent views over Loch Earn. The bleak and rocky character of Glen Ogle so enthralled Anderson that he described it as 'the Khyber Pass' of Scotland – with permissible hyperbole, given his devotion

to the railway, and his desire that others should enjoy its beauty. Glen Ogle gave its name to the listed 12-arch viaduct which has become a highlight on National Cycle Network Route 7.

A branch line opening in 1886 was built to serve Killin by Loch Tay. It left the main line at Killin Junction, high on a hillside, affording views of at least three surrounding peaks. After the final passing loop and station at Luib, trains arrived at Crianlarich which became a junction with the opening of the West Highland Railway between Glasgow and Fort William in 1894. It was construction of a connection between the two lines in 1897 which allowed the eastern part of the C&O to be closed, routeing trains between Glasgow and Oban over the West Highland and the still-open western part of the C&O.

Few railway lines had locomotives that took the name of the line for which they were designed, but the

Above: Oban apart, Callander station was the largest on the line after reconstruction in a vaguely Swiss style in 1883. The site is now a car-park.

Left: LMS Class Five 4-6-0 No. 45356 drifts down Glen Ogle with an Oban to Glasgow Buchanan Street train *c.*1956.

C&O had two. The first 'Oban Bogies' were 4-4-0s with stovepipe chimneys, inclined cylinders and rounded cabs, and had small four-wheel tenders so that they would fit on the short turntable at Oban. A larger turntable had been installed by the time John McIntosh designed the second class of nine 'Oban Bogies': the '55' class 4-6-0s, which were the first inside-cylinder six-coupled bogie engines in Scotland.

It was common practice in the 19th and early 20th centuries for drivers to have 'their own' engine, in which they took greater pride and could extract better performance than was possible under a common-user regime. The C&O, like the Caledonian, went one better with goods guards having their own brake vans. One Callander guard had curtains on the windows and a polished waxcloth on the floor, and was so indignant when he found it dirty one day that he complained to the district superintendent. It was suggested that he might have left the van unlocked, allowing it to have been entered by a cat. The offended guard retorted: 'Sir, you are mistaken. I have yet to meet the cat that can tear two pages out of the working timetable.'

Care beyond the call of duty extended to C&O stations. As a writer in the *Railway Magazine* of 1941 wrote: '...the prettiest stations in the Highland hills have long been those on the Callander & Oban...[with some] embellishments, such as leaden storks supporting fountain nozzles, but the real charm of these stations lies in their smallness, their gardens, and their lovely situations.'

The line was already earmarked for closure when, in October 1965, a landslide near Glenoglehead blocked the line and brought about its premature end. Parts of the trackbed have been subsumed by a road, and others converted into walking and cycling routes.

Below: A former Caledonian Railway '439' class 0-4-4T No. 55204 climbs through Glen Ogle with the 4.05pm Callander to Killin school train. The later stovepipe chimney did nothing for their appearance.

LISTOWEL & BALLYBUNION RAILWAY

IN A COUNTRY blessed with more than its fair share of idiosyncratic railways, Ireland's Listowel & Ballybunion Railway (LBR) in County Kerry won the laurels. The best-known of 19th-century monorails has spawned many stories mocking its impracticality, but it was one of the most visited and photographed of Irish railways because of its demonstration of Charles Lartigue's monorail principles.

Though called a monorail, Lartigue's system used three rails: a raised centre running rail mounted on A-framed trestles, and two mid-trestle rails to prevent oscillation. Its virtue was claimed to be cheapness of construction, since liberties could be taken in preparing the trackbed. Its drawbacks were added complexity in the mechanism required to switch tracks, the awkwardness of having locomotives, carriages and wagons that straddled the centre running rail, and the conundrum of how to cross a road.

The 9¼-mile (14.8km) line was authorized in 1886 and officially opened on Leap Year Day in 1888, though most of that time was spent acquiring the land; construction took just five months. The line linked the County Kerry seaside resort of Ballybunion with Listowel station on the Great Western & Southern Railway Tralee–Limerick line. There was a single intermediate station with a loop and siding at Lisselton. Ballybunion station was equipped

Opposite: The girl might well look at the idiosyncratic locomotive waiting to leave Listowel station, for there was nothing else like it in the British Isles. It ran with 'a happy disregard for punctuality'.

with a goods shed and sidings, and the line continued for a short distance past the church to the shore for loading sand.

Three dark green-liveried locomotives, based on a design by the French mechanical engineer Anatole Mallet, were built by Hunslet of Leeds. Two locomotives were housed at the Ballybunion headquarters and the third at Listowel for the first train out in the morning. The driver was on one side of the running rail, and the fireman on the other.

The only months when the railway made a profit were during the summer – when the population of the seaside resort of Ballybunion swelled from 300 to 3,000, thanks to the excellent bathing. Apart from the carriage of general merchandise, the L&B brought sea sand inland for use as top dressing. Though the railway had a horse box and two cattle trucks, livestock traffic seems to have been negligible, perhaps because farmers considered the distance between Ballybunion and Listowel to be so modest that it was not worth the expense of getting the railway to take their beasts to market. More telling might be the logistical difficulty of moving one animal, which naturally required a balancing load.

The story is told of the tribulations of conveying a piano; this entailed borrowing two calves to provide the means of a balanced return working. Another tale, perhaps apocryphal, is related by Fergus Mulligan: a farmer 'bought a cow at Listowel and borrowed another for the train trip to Ballybunion. A second animal was then needed to return the first one borrowed and so the business went on for most of that day until he had lost

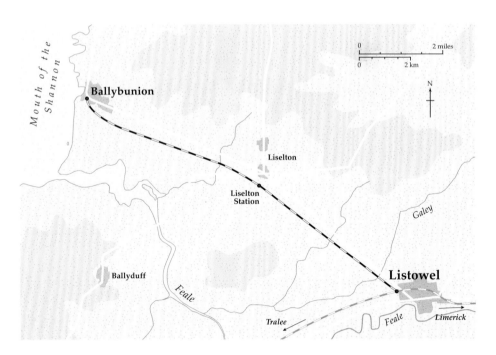

Opposite above: Ballybunion station in 1890 with the engine shed above the man leaning against the A-framed trestle.

Opposite below: The three locomotives were painted dark green. The tenders had an additional pair of cylinders but they were apparently not used.

Below: The railway achieved fame way beyond its significance for the local economy.

his own cow, acquired two he did not want and owed the company a small fortune in freight charges.'

Road crossings entailed a rotating section of track or a canal-pattern double drawbridge operated by chains and pulleys, of a complexity that would have delighted W. Heath Robinson. There were 40 crossings of one sort or another on the line, and a silent 9.5mm Pathé film survives showing a donkey and cart negotiating one. Steps were provided at the end of some of the carriages so that passengers could cross the line.

A visitor in 1917 was not impressed by the view from the carriage window: 'there is nothing to be seen beyond peat land and scrub'; and *The Engineer* reported that the line passed 'through deep bogs and bad ground generally'. Nor did passengers take kindly to the noise generated by the rail behind their heads, seating being back-to-back. By 1897 the line was bankrupt and placed in the hands of a receiver, but it struggled on through the next two decades. During the Civil War, there were various acts of sabotage, and the frequency of mail robberies prompted the suspension of services for a period. The last straw came in 1924 when it was not included in the creation of Great Southern Railways, making closure inevitable. The

last train ran on 14 October, and the line was dismantled with great thoroughness by T. W. Ward of Sheffield.

A suggestion was even made in the London *Evening News* that an engine from the railway should be preserved in the Victoria and Albert Museum to illustrate engineering progress. Nothing came of it, but in 2003 a ²/₃ mile (1km) section of Lartigue monorail was opened on the trackbed of the line in Listowel. It is worked by a diesel-engined replica of one of the original locomotives built by Alan Keef.

Above: Locomotive No. 1 soon after arrival on the railway to judge from its numberplate on the tender – they were soon transferred to the cab sides. The two boilers were designed to use coal but an experiment was made with peat in 1917.

Opposite above: The steps at the end of a carriage to allow the line to be crossed being demonstrated at Ballybunion station with the castle ruins on the right.

Opposite below: The L&B attracted many visitors for its curiosity value, as here at Ballybunion station.

CHARLES FRANÇOIS MARIE-THÉRÈSE LARTIGUE

Charles Lartigue (1834-1907) was born in Toulouse and developed his idea for a monorail while engineer to a large farm in South Oran, Algeria. Inspiration came from caravans of camels carrying loads in balanced baskets on their flanks. He created a 37.5km (60-mile) horse- or camel-drawn monorail on A-framed supports which was both untroubled by shifting sands and easily moved to different areas where the alfa, or esparto grass, was being harvested.

Lartigue took out his first patent in 1882 and two years later demonstrated an electrically powered line in Paris. More followed, but the only other major application of his principles was a 16km (10-mile) line in the Loire, from Feurs to Panissières, though it never opened to the public and lasted only a few years before being scrapped. A proposal was also made to build the Lynton & Barnstaple Railway in Devon as a monorail on the Lartigue system.

ASIA

PATIALA STATE MONORAIL TRAINWAY

THE HISTORY OF RAILWAYS is full of eccentric engineering cul-de-sacs, from Brunel's atmospheric system to dozens of bizarre monorail proposals. Among the more credible of the latter – and one that at least saw the light of day – was the Ewing System, whose principal manifestation was the Patiala State Monorail Trainway in the Punjab. This short-lived creation would have been all but forgotten were it not for the extraordinary survival of its locomotives, one of which is now in the National Rail Museum in New Delhi.

The Ewing System's adoption for the transport needs of the State of Patiala was due to Colonel C.W. Bowles. He had used Ewing-style monorails for building projects at the railway workshops and associated township at Kharagpur in Bengal in the 1900s. The system placed 95 per cent of the weight of the vehicle on the single rail, with the remainder on the balance wheel to the side. Little is known about W.J. Ewing himself except that he lived at Barrackpore in Bengal and later in Madras, and that for some reason his US patent of 1895 gives his name as Charles Ewing.

By chance, Bowles visited the Sikh state of Patiala and met its ruler, the Maharaja Sir Bhupinder Singh. They got on so well that before 1907 Bowles had become State Engineer. One of the state's obligations was to maintain a sizeable contingent of mules and muleteers as part of

Imperial Service Troops in support of the Indian Army. Rather than keep them in idleness, it was decided they could fulfil the need for better transport by hauling monorail vehicles.

Accordingly, Bowles contracted a Bombay engineering company to build and operate two lines. The first was the 15-mile (24km) route from the North Western Railway (NWR) station at Sirhind to Morinda, with two intermediate stations; its first section, as far as Bassi, opened in February 1907. Bowles's papers recorded that in one month the four passenger vehicles carried 20,000 passengers, though 15 wagons were also fitted up with knifeboard (back-to-back) seating. In addition, there was a superior saloon with a washbasin and end balconies, which is presumed to have been Col. Bowles's inspection carriage. Most vehicles had two double-flanged wheels and a single balance wheel on an outrigger arm, though there were also some bogie vehicles with two balance wheels for longer loads. Apart from occasional experiments with horses, the line was worked by mules until its closure in 1927, brought about by construction of the NWR's Sirhind–Rupar line.

The other line was intended to link the NWR goods yard at Patiala with Sunam, but there is doubt whether the final section beyond Bhawanigarh was ever built. The monorail had to cross the NWR on the level – an exceptionally unusual circumstance – and the rails were notched to allow the passage of the flanges. The monorail was laid in the soft shoulders of a surfaced road so that the balance wheel ran along the metalled part. Had the full line been built, it would have been 40 miles (64km)

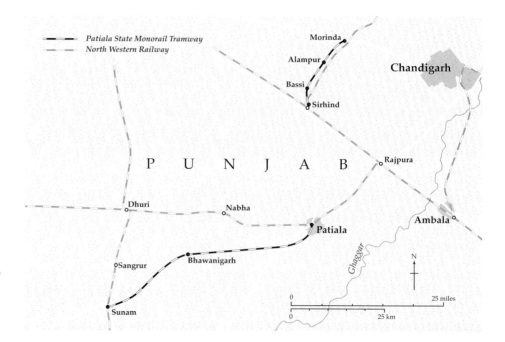

Below: A photograph probably taken when Michael Satow visited the derelict remains of the Patiala State Monorail in the early 1970s, during his search for objects for the railway museum in New Delhi.

long, which probably prompted an order for four 0-3-0 steam locomotives from Orenstein & Koppel in Berlin at a cost of £500–600. They appear to have been finished in a green livery reminiscent of London & North Eastern Railway locomotives.

The locomotives' centre driving wheel was flangeless, and the firebox was fired on the right-hand side, facilitated by an extended cab. The 63cm (25in) diameter boiler was fitted with a very tall stovepipe chimney, and supplied steam to two outside cylinders. It was intended to use the steam locomotives on both lines and we know that they worked the one mile (1.6km) from Patiala to City Mandi, but it is unlikely that we can ever answer whether they operated only on the longer line, or both, and even whether they ventured beyond City Mandi. The lighter rail used on the shorter Morinda line suggests that locomotives would have been confined to the Bhawanigarh route. This had closed by about 1914, due to competition from 'the motor-road tongas and wagonettes' according to Bowles, but also to wood-boring insects snacking on the sleepers (iron had been used on the Morinda line).

Equipment, including the locomotives, from the Bhawanigarh line was offered for sale in trade journals in 1921 and 1925, but they remained unsold in Patiala, almost forgotten in their open-sided sheds. A visitor to Sunam in the 1960s found that the stationmaster there had never even heard of the monorail. A reminder of it appeared in the 1957 book *Unusual Railways*, and in a subsequent article by one of its authors, J.R. Day, in the *Railway World* in 1962. This appears to have alerted the man charged with finding artefacts for the railway museum being set up in Delhi, Michael Satow. He had worked in various senior positions for ICI in India for a decade, and on his retirement combed the country for appropriate items to tell the story of the development of railways in India. His search was the subject of a BBC *The World About Us* documentary in 1975.

Remarkably, the locomotive rescued for the museum was restored to working order by the Northern Railway workshops at Amritsar, and a 0.4km (¼-mile) loop laid around the museum grounds on which to demonstrate it. Another locomotive was restored in a maroon livery and placed on a plinth at Amritsar.

Above: The restored locomotive receiving attention in its shed at the National Rail Museum in New Delhi.

MAHARAJA SIR BHUPINDER SINGH

Born in 1891, Bhupinder Singh became the ruling Maharaja of the princely state of Patiala from 1900 until his death in 1938. He was captain of the Indian cricket team which visited England in 1911, and was on the General Staff in France, Belgium, Italy and Palestine during the First World War. He was the first man in India to own an aircraft and had an airstrip built at Patiala. Col. Bowles had a high regard for him and felt his death so keenly – he happened to be on home leave in England at the time – that he did not have the heart to return to India. His photographs of the monorail remained in India and were lost.

BOSTAN–FORT SANDEMAN (NOW ZHOB)

MANY RAILWAYS BUILT by colonial powers had at least a partial military or strategic objective, but few had so specific a purpose as the 2ft 6in (762mm) gauge line built in the North West Frontier Province of India (now Pakistan) between Khanai and Fort Sandeman. Construction by Baluchistan Chrome Mines Ltd began in 1916 during the First World War to carry chrome ore from its mine at Hindubagh, which was shipped to Britain for use in munitions factories. But what attracted small numbers of travellers and photographers to the railway in later years was the wild mountainous country through which it ran, and its exceptional length for a narrow-gauge railway.

The first 46¼ miles (74km) to Hindubagh officially opened as an 'assisted siding' in September 1917, but many give an opening date of 1921 when the line became part of the North Western Railway. By the time the line had been extended to Kila Saifulla in 1927 and Fort Sandeman in 1929, it was 280km (175 miles) long, making it one of the longest railways of this gauge in the world. It also reached the highest point of any railway in India: 7,221ft (2,201m) at Kan Mehtarzai. The Zhob Valley Railway (ZVR), as it became known, might have become even longer had the original proposal been realised to extend it to Bannu, terminus of another narrow-gauge line from Mari Indus.

Opposite: Against a backdrop of the rugged hills that form the border between Pakistan and Afghanistan near Bostan, GS class 2-8-2 No. 65 heaves its train of chrome ore empties away from the junction.

Because the journey between its termini took about 19 hours, at an average speed of 9mph (14.7km/h), the ZVR was one of the few narrow-gauge railways in the world with sleeping cars. The railway may have lacked profitable traffic apart from the chrome ore, but it became important in the life of the Zhob Valley, even having the rare distinction of a four-wheel mobile dispensary carriage. One of the problems was that the local tribes considered it part of their birthright to travel on the train free of charge, never thinking to visit the ticket window in the distinctive octagonal room that formed part of the ticket office at the 11 stations.

Moreover, the line ran through one of the most desolate and sparsely populated parts of the country. The 1901 census of the district served by the ZVR revealed that the population density across 9,626 square miles (24,931sq km) was just seven per square mile. The only town was Fort Sandeman, where a garrison was set up in 1889 and named after Sir Robert Sandeman, who had established a degree of peace during the late 19th century. The railway carried the cereals and rice that formed the area's main crops, and the mulberries, apricots, pomegranates and grapes that grew in the upper parts of the valley.

It was one of the few lines in India where snow was a problem, and locomotives were fitted with a small plough in winter. A sapper on a surveying party in 1890–1 for a railway from Quetta to Dera Ismail Khan recalled the piercing wind, and how at Mehtarzai 'basins of water in our tents were found frozen solid every morning'. During the winter of 1970 a train got stuck in a 6ft (2m) drift.

Left: Locomotives on the narrow gauge in Pakistan were generally well maintained, as evidenced by the condition of G class 2-8-2 No. 58, built in 1909 by the North British Locomotive Co. in Glasgow.

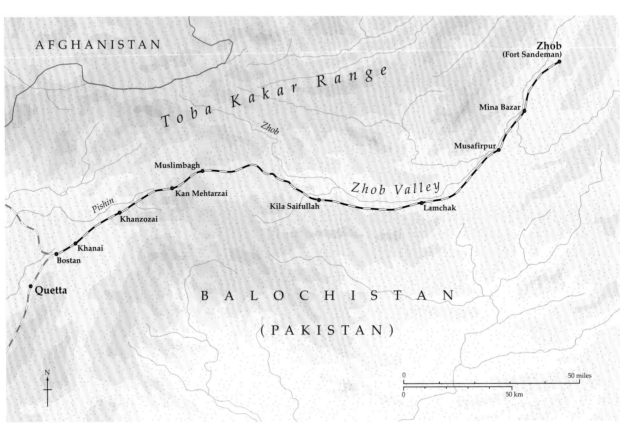

In 1939 the line was extended in a westerly direction from Khanai by creating interlaced dual-gauge track for 10 miles (16km) to provide better connections at Bostan Junction, and the workshops and engine shed at Khanai were moved to Bostan. An elevated loading stage was built to facilitate the transfer of chrome ore from narrow- to broad-gauge wagons. In the 1960s Hindubagh became Muslimbagh, but Fort Sandeman retained its name until 1976 when Prime Minister Bhutto changed it to Zhob ('bubbling water').

The sight of the chrome trains heading east from Bostan to the mines was unforgettable. At each end of a train of bogie hopper wagons would be one of the oil-burning G class 2-8-2s, roaring away as they began the climb of 2,658ft (810m) in 56 miles (89.6km). The setting of snow-dusted mountains rising out of the valley's rugged slopes, the crystal-clear air, and the sound of the locomotives, their exhaust in and out of syncopation, made it a captivating experience. The G class no longer had age on their side in the final years; all but six had been built before the end of the First World War, the majority by North British in Glasgow and just four by Nasmyth, Wilson in Manchester. (take back line)

Passenger services ended in 1985 but the chrome traffic continued for another year or two. There was a flutter of hope in 1999 when the locomotives were spruced up at the behest of Railways Minister Yaqub Nasir, who saw a future for the ZVR as a tourist attraction for his native Baluchistan. Nothing came of it, and the track was officially lifted in 2007–8 though much had already disappeared, as a local report made clear: 'On account of law and order situation the track was difficult to monitor and a huge amount had already been spent on deputing the staff who sometime felt helpless in the hands of Local tribal people. Theft of track was an ongoing process and a considerable length of track had been plundered by the steel hungry thieves.'

A proposal was made in 2016 to rebuild the railway as a broad-gauge line between Bostan and Kola Jam Bhakkar under the China-Pakistan Economic Corridor, with Bostan–Zhob as the first stage.

Below: G class 2-8-2 No. 46, built by North British Locomotive Co. in Glasgow in 1911, provides banking assistance on the climb to Khanai, against the impressive mountains that flank the Zhob Valley.

SURABAYA STEAM TRAM

MANY TOWNS AND cities which had tram lines built during the 19th century relied on steam until replaced by electric traction in the early years of the 20th. By the First World War, steam-worked tram lines were rare, and they tended to be those which were more rural than urban, such as the Wisbech & Upwell Tramway in East Anglia and the Glyn Valley Tramway in Wales. Other survivors could be found in the Dutch East Indies, now Indonesia.

At the eastern end of Java lies Surabaya, one of Southeast Asia's oldest port cities and once the largest city in the Dutch East Indies. Those who have come across the place have usually done so through the song 'Surabaya Johnny' in *Happy End*, the musical comedy by Kurt Weill, Elisabeth Hauptmann, and Bertolt Brecht. But a few remember the world's last urban steam tram which shrieked its way through the streets and markets of a city straight out of a novel by Somerset Maugham.

The tramway was built by a company set up in Holland in 1886, the tongue-twisting Naamloze Vennootschap Oost Java Stoomtram Maatschappij (NV. OJS), to build tram lines in Java. The company won the concession for Surabaya and built a two-line 88km (55-mile) network through the city and out into the country, the first line opening in September 1890. The two lines linked Ujung and Sepanjang via Pasar Turi and Tanjung Perak and Staatsspoor. Other tram lines were electrified from 1923, though paradoxically the last electric line closed in 1969, leaving the steam tram as the only surviving route, running from Wonokromo to the docks at Udjang where the ferries from Madura docked.

Tram engines were used on various rural branch lines, but the only other urban steam tram in the Dutch East Indies was in Semerang. Though built by a different company, the two systems shared the same design of tram engine, the B12 0-4-0T. Most were built by Beyer, Peacock of Manchester which supplied 99 tram engines to Java between 1882 and 1910, though a smaller number was made by Werkspoor of Amsterdam in 1902–3 and four were built at Semerang Works in 1922–3. Some of the Semarang engines were transferred to Surabaya following electrification of the lines under the Dutch, and when Indonesia became independent in 1949 there were 46 B12 tram engines left in the country.

The main station on the Surabaya steam tram and the site of the railway's workshop and four-road engine shed were at Wonokromo-Kota. The size of the shed reflects the capacity and utility of the tram system between the world wars: in 1930 the steam-worked lines alone carried 5,797,438 passengers – a daily average of 15,883.

Daybreak would see wafts of pale wood smoke emanating from the shed area, and street vendors arriving with all manner of goods, from chickens to children's whirligigs, to be taken to market. Waiting passengers would shelter under the station's overall roof prior to boarding the four-wheel coaches. With a quick whistle the light blue tram engine would slide into motion, all its moving parts hidden by skirts to prevent mishap, and then give a much longer blast before crossing the first road of the journey and beginning its daily battle with obstructions.

The track's curves sometimes limited the crew's sight-lines, and abrupt halts were often necessary as a bend was rounded to find a lorry blocking an open level crossing. Indifference to the tram by vehicles

Opposite: B12 0-4-0 B1221, built by Beyer, Peacock in Manchester in 1884, weaves through a street near Kebonradja.

and pedestrians compelled frequent and prolonged use of the piercing high-pitched whistle. The only segregated section of track was along the middle of a dual carriageway, but the real fun started as the tram began to thread the rabbit warren of houses and stalls built to within a whisker of the train. Moments before the train passed, the track was invisible, covered in a jumble of rickshaws, bedsteads, birdcages, sweet stalls and cooking stoves which parted like the bow-wave of a ship and immediately closed behind it.

It was much easier to shut the tram down than impose order on anarchic traffic, and that happened in 1978. Today levels of congestion and pollution in Surabaya have prompted proposals to create a new 17km (10½-mile) line from Wonokromo in the south to Sono Kembang.

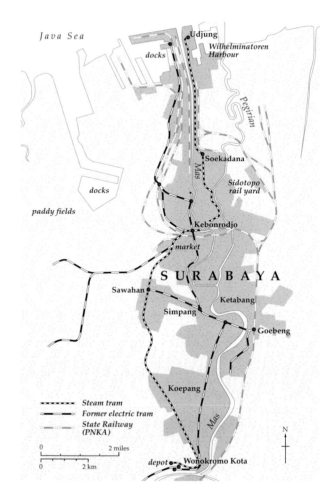

Below: Wonokromo-Kota station was the most important station on the Surabaya steam tram, with an overall roof – a rare facility for an urban tram. Tram engines also worked some country lines in Java.

Above: The colourful market at Benteng rather than the ferry terminal for Madura became the destination of the tram in the final years.

Left: Cycle rickshaws known as becaks were more common on the streets of Surabaya than cars when B1221 headed for Benteng near Kebonradja, on 7 August 1975.

THE HEJAZ RAILWAY

FEW RAILWAYS HAVE gained such a mystique as the main line of the Hejaz Railway, inseparable from the exploits of Colonel T.E. Lawrence in disrupting Turkish troop movements during the First World War. Even without David Lean's 1962 epic film *Lawrence of Arabia*, Lawrence would be a household name. Though the railway eventually stretched for 1,305km (815²/₃ miles) from Damascus Kanawat station to Medina, it was incomplete and never fulfilled its original purpose of providing a link between the capital of the Ottoman Empire at Constantinople and the holy city of Mecca. Though trains did carry pilgrims en route to the Hajj for less than a decade, the railway's most important role became the supply of Turkish forces and equipment.

It was conceived as a means of stemming the suffering and death toll on pilgrims who crossed the desert and Hejaz Mountains to reach Mecca. Less openly spoken were strategic considerations and the desire for a public-works project that would bolster Ottoman prestige. The first suggestion for a railway was in 1864, but it was not until 1900 that the order to begin was given by Sultan Abdul Hamid II, with the German Turkish-speaking Oberingenieur Heinrich August Meissner in charge for most of the construction period. That year, the British Consul at Damascus had to write to the ambassador in Constantinople to apologize for not informing him of this development; it had seemed to him and others 'so wildly improbable, not to say fantastic, that I refrained from reporting on it to your Excellency'. The Consul's attitude

was an understandable one, if the challenges of water alone are considered.

Money to build the railway came from a combination of an early form of crowd funding – voluntary contributions from Muslims all over the world – and taxes, including a single levy of 10 per cent of one month's pay for Turkish officials. Though concurrent with work on the Berlin–Baghdad railway, and sharing its objective of strengthening the Ottoman Empire's hold over its Arab provinces, the Hejaz Railway was quite separate.

An intention to frustrate the train movements of an aggressor by choosing a different track gauge from a neighbouring country is thought to have been behind a number of decisions which have damaged the peacetime economics of railways. Some writers have stated that the Hejaz's unusual gauge of 1050mm (3ft 5¼in) is a case in point, but its selection was motivated not by strategic considerations, but by the hope that the railway's first part would be formed by buying the French-built Damascus to Muzeirib line. Not only was this line 1050mm gauge, but so was another French route, from Beirut to Damascus, by which the Hejaz intended to receive its locomotives and rolling stock.

Though construction began at Muzeirib on this basis in 1900, relations deteriorated, partly because of high charges for deliveries. To end dependence on the French, the Hejaz built its own railway south from Damascus to Dera'a, and a railway from Haifa to Dera'a. The latter entailed some outstanding engineering between its low point of 238m (780ft) below sea level at the crossing of the River Jordan – the lowest railway in the world – and the climb out of the Yarmuk Valley. From Dera'a the Hejaz made for Amman and Ma'an before turning south-east towards Medina and Mecca. The exit from Amman also

Opposite: The station building and goods shed at Ma'an c.1910 with a Hartmann 2-8-2 on a goods train. Meissener Pasha based himself in the house on the right.

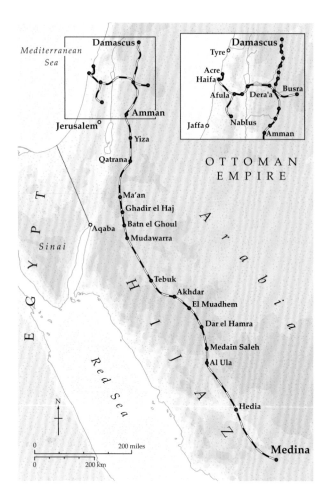

required heavy earthworks and one of the line's most impressive structures, a double-tiered viaduct. Turkish soldiers worked on the trackbed and laid the permanent way while Italians under contract built the bridges and station buildings. The soldiers also had to defend the works against determined Arab attacks.

Even though much of the line was built across desert sand, it was decided that the risk from flash floods would be mitigated by laying the track on an embankment about one metre high. The first workforce was so badly treated that there was a mutiny, and its Chief of Construction was court-martialled. His successor handled the workforce and logistics more successfully and eventually developed a good working relationship with Heinrich Meissner, but there were serious problems as such as dysentery,

scurvy and outbreaks of cholera in 1902–3, when many employees died or fled the workings. Openings of sections of line were timed to fall on 1 September, whether or not the line was really finished, because it marked the anniversary of the Sultan's accession.

By the end of 1907 a trip that would have taken three weeks before the railway had been reduced to three days, encouraging 25,000 single journeys that year. The prospect of faster and more comfortable journeys to the holy cities 'aroused the enthusiasm of Moslems in every part of the world except the Hedjaz', as one writer put it. It was said that half the local Arab tribes lived from arranging caravans to Mecca from its nearest port at Jeddah and the other half from plundering them. When preliminary work was started on the last 432km (270 miles) south of Medina, using only Muslim labour to prevent infidels approaching Mecca, the Bedouin tribesmen massacred the construction workers and the project was abandoned. The final section to Medina was built quickly and opened to a splendidly ornate station in 1908. However, the haste and an absence of skilled labour, due to the ban on infidel workers, resulted in several locomotives derailing.

The engines ordered for the railway were a mix of 2-6-0, 2-8-0 and, later, 2-8-2 tender locomotives with various tank engines in wheel arrangements ranging from 0-6-0 to 0-10-0, from German and Swiss makers. Most carriages came from Belgium, and the freight stock included flat wagons, each with two iron water tanks for station and guardhouse supplies.

Construction was abandoned following the Young Turk Revolution of 1908 which ended Abdul Hamid's autocracy and restored the constitution, though the attacks by Bedouin tribes also discouraged further extension. A report in January 1911 recorded that at least 16 stations had been destroyed, several carriages burnt and an engine or two 'badly injured'. Lawrence would find willing allies among the Arabs who had viewed the railway as a symbol of Ottoman hegemony as well as a threat to their livelihoods.

Besides pilgrims and troops, the line carried a heavy traffic in grain for the cities and export through Haifa,

Above: The climb out of Amman provided an impressive spectacle, here with 2-8-2 No. 71, built by the Belgian manufacturer Forges, Usines et Fonderies à Haine Saint Pierre in 1956.

as well as smaller tonnages of flour, fruit and vegetables, wood, petrol and coal. Unfortunately, maintenance of every aspect of the railway was so poor that cancelled trains or late running was endemic. Constant attacks on permanent-way gangs and the fortified stations made matters worse.

The Arab Revolt against the Turks during the First World War began in June 1916, but the railway suffered no more inconvenience than a few removed rails and piles of stones on the track. Dynamite supplied by Britain to the Arabs had been returned as being 'too dangerous'. The revolt was on the point of collapse when Lawrence began his indeterminate mission in October 1916. His attacks on trains and bridges initially took place south of Ma'an, and targeted the supply line to the main Turkish garrison in the Hejaz at Medina, a stronghold of 14,000 experienced troops with artillery. Seats on wartime Hejaz trains were priced according to their distance from the locomotive, the cheapest being placed right behind it.

Above: The numberplate of No. 53, a 2-8-2 built by Arnold Jung Lokomotivfabrik of Kirchen in Rheinland-Pfalz in 1955.

Above: Five 4-6-2 locomotives built in 1953 for Thailand by Nippon Sharyo in Japan came to the Hejaz; No. 82, is seen here climbing through the suburbs of Amman with a train in autumn 1985.

A reminder of Lawrence's time sabotaging Turkish supply lines was brought back to England. He kept in his college rooms at All Souls, Oxford, where he had been awarded a seven-year Fellowship, the station bell from Tel Shahm, 548 km (342½ miles) south-east of Damascus. He captured the souvenir on 19 April 1918, when a dawn attack on the station with a Bedouin contingent succeeded in surprising the Turkish troops, who surrendered without a fight. Lawrence claimed the bell, while others took the ticket punch and office stamp.

After the First World War, a service of sorts was revived, with diversions around blown bridges, but there is a record of a rare pilgrim train taking 12 days to travel between Medina and Ma'an. Heavy rains and conflict between Arab factions in 1924 brought an end to the short-lived 843km (527-mile) section of the railway south of Ma'an. It had some spectacular and rugged sections as the line climbed to a 1,128m (3,700ft) summit at Batn el Ghoul ('the Devil's Belly') and descended from a wild chasm by a series of horseshoe curves. Medain Saleh became something of a railway town, with repair shops, engine shed, a double water tower and houses for railway staff. The oasis of Al-`Ula was supported by 'copious springs and 1,000 acres [405ha] planted with date palms and cereals', as a 1913 traveller described it. It was also the station at which infidels had to end their southerly journey.

After the war, ownership of the railway was divided between France and Britain and the subject of constant diplomatic negotiation. There was a weekly service between Amman and Ma'an and a daily service between Damascus and Haifa. During the Second World War, the railway was in the hands of the Allies once the Vichy French forces had been defeated in 1941.

Talks between Syria, Jordan and Saudi Arabia about rebuilding the railway began in 1948, but it was not until 1960 that a contract was drawn up with an unlikely consortium of Arabian, Japanese and Spanish companies. This was cancelled in 1962, and a British consortium took over the following year, carrying out much work south of Ma'an before political and financial difficulties brought the project to a halt in 1971. Today the only regular traffic is phosphate over a new line to the port of Aqaba in Jordan, and given the war in Syria, it is unlikely that any other part of the Hejaz Railway will see another train.

Below: During the last decades of the 20th century, most trains over the Hejaz in Jordan were charters for railway photographers. On such an occasion in 1985, Haine Saint Pierre 2-8-2 No. 71 leaves one of the few tunnels on the railway on the outskirts of Amman.

AUSTRALASIA

THE GHAN: CENTRAL AUSTRALIA RAILWAY

MANY OF THE RAILWAYS in this book traversed desolate country, but few can match the one that forged a route through the 'red centre' of Australia to link the south and north coasts. Today's Ghan train between Adelaide and Darwin travels over a standard-gauge line via Port Augusta, Tarcoola and Coober Pedy, but the original Ghan took a more easterly route on tracks 3ft 6in (1067mm) apart. There are various stories about how the train gained its name, but they all relate to the Afghan cameleers whose strings of imported animals supplied the country between Port Augusta and Oodnadatta – until they were displaced by the gradual opening of the railway between Port Augusta and Alice Springs over the 50 years from 1879 to 1929.

Demand for what became the Central Australia Railway was fuelled by unrealistic optimism over the land's potential for wheat, encouraged by a few bountiful harvests around 1870. Wheat and the need for a transcontinental railway dominated the public mind, and the reasoned caution of South Australia's Surveyor-General, George Goyder, about the prospects for cereal production was scorned. Goyder's Line, indicating the northern boundary of land that received an annual average of 10 inches, was dismissed by the South Australian government, triggering a northward land movement.

The 3,200km Overland Telegraph Line between Port Augusta and Darwin opened in 1872, creating a telegraph link between London and Adelaide. The railway, authorized four years later, was to parallel the route of the telegraph, which had one of its repeater stations at Alice Springs (then named Stuart). The line was to be built in stages, and the surveyors began prospecting from Port Augusta on Spencer Gulf, mindful of the interests of wheat farmers.

The result was a route further east through more difficult terrain, requiring the use of dynamite, which had recently been invented by Alfred Nobel. The first sod was turned in 1878, with Chinese labour forming part of the construction gangs on a project that contemporaries compared with America's Union Pacific. A dozen ships brought equipment from Britain, including Beyer, Peacock locomotives from Manchester. The first section opened for goods between Port Augusta and Quorn in 1879, with an inaugural consignment of flour from Quorn's mill.

Reports of harsh working conditions for construction workers hampered recruitment; some said they would rather starve on the streets of Melbourne than endure the privations of the Outback. As construction progressed, the run of good seasons ended and faith in a prosperous farming future diminished, along with belief in the old wives' tale that rain followed the plough. Government Gums (or Farina) was reached in 1882, and Hergott (or Marree) in 1884 when construction was resumed, primarily to relieve the unemployment that was fuelling emigration from South Australia. One can well imagine the thoughts of urban waiters, clerks and even

Opposite: One of the first trains at Woolshed Flat station between Port Augusta and Quorn, to judge from the pose. Today the station is on the heritage Pichi Richi Railway and equipped with a turning wye.

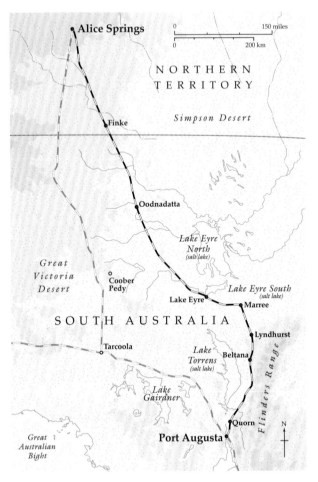

watch repairers as they experienced their first taste of the Outback's rigours and heat. The explorer of the continent's interior, Charles Sturt, wrote of ink that dried on the nib, and fingernails that cracked like glass.

By 1891 the head of steel had reached Oodnadatta, and there it remained for the next 38 years. Despite Hergott entraining 15,651 steers and 20,093 sheep in 1892, the railway ran at a huge loss, and periodic calls for the original vision to be fulfilled often died out in a squabble over the best route. Not until 1926 was a decision taken to press on to Alice, but engineering difficulties and sand drift delayed the arrival of the first train from Adelaide until 6 August 1929. On board was a party of scientists from the state capital's university, intent on collecting facts about the disappearing tribes of the Centre.

The initial train service reflected the sparse population served by the line. A limited-stop train with dining- and sleeping-cars ran once a fortnight, and the mixed trains operated to a schedule that calls to mind Mark Twain's quip about fitting a cowcatcher to the guard's van instead of the engine. But a major source of traffic was Queensland's beef cattle, which were driven to railheads in 'mobs' already graded by size to minimize the risk of injury on the railway journey. Drovers' reputations depended on losing few beasts en route, and punctuality in arriving at the waiting trains. No sooner

Right: Taken in August 1953, this NM class 4-8-0 leaving Alice Springs for Adelaide with the Ghan must have been one of the last steam workings. The 22 NMs dated from 1925–7 and all were built by Thompson & Co. at Castlemaine, Victoria.

Above: An early train hauled by a Y class 2-6-0 with four-wheel tender crossing the Waukarie Creek bridge near Woolshed Flat, c.1890. Three builders constructed 129 Ys in 1885–98.

had the railway opened to Alice than 3,000 head of cattle owned by Sir Sidney Kidman arrived, requiring 12 trains for the journey south.

Rather cack-handed efforts were made to develop tourism, such as the offer of a three-week tour, at £65, for men. A visit to the MacDonnell Ranges by the wife of the Governor of Victoria, Lady Somers, convinced the railway authorities that perhaps women could cope with the privations of the Outback, and they agreed to accept bookings from the fair sex. Numbers grew, though the sardonic complaint by one hotel keeper – 'They come with a 10 pound note and one shirt and don't change

either' – suggests that the benefits to the local economy were limited.

A journey on the old Ghan was something of a lottery. Progress, slow at the best of times, could be impeded by bushfires, drifting sand or clouds of grasshoppers which prevented the locomotive finding its feet on slippery rails. It wasn't uncommon for wheels to part company with the rails, perhaps where termites had dined on the sleepers, but what really worried train crews were clouds, especially after steam power gave way to diesel. Torrential rain could create flash floods that marooned trains for days, even weeks. A steam locomotive could cope with a greater depth of water than a diesel, which could only manage a few inches.

The wisdom of the route chosen for the section north of Oodnadatta was called into question by the disruption caused by the Finke River 'running a banker'. When this occurred, normally placid streams could widen to five miles. On one occasion, after the Finke had stopped a train, a member of the crew swam to the other side of the river, and managed to attach a wire rope between trees on each bank. The driver and fireman then went across on a 'flying fox' rope swing, found a gangers' trolley, and headed into Rumbalara where they lit up an engine and returned with a coach. Once the flood had abated sufficiently to allow a trolley across, the passengers were ferried over the water and continued their journey to Alice.

Some passengers relished this as part of the adventure, but other such Indiana Jones-type exploits ended with relief by air. In 1963, 114 passengers had to be airlifted from carriage roofs, and a 'minor Berlin airlift' was required in 1967 when the railway was shut for 27 days following 32 breaches of the track. The crew once resorted to shooting a consignment of goats to keep the passengers alive until former bombers dropped canvas bags of provisions.

The ability of train crews to improvise repairs or cope with an incident drew admiration from passengers. One late afternoon in 1954, a train derailed on dodgy track but everything remained upright. Knowing it would be a while before rescue, the driver gathered up some scrub and wood and suggested the passengers have a sing-song around the fire, accompanied by a passenger who had been playing the banjo when the train derailed and hadn't even noticed what had happened. The dining-car dispensed food and drinks, and a considerate passenger went up to the driver and asked if he would like a beer. 'No thanks,' he replied, 'I don't drink on duty but I could do with a brandy.'

During the Second World War, after the Army occupied Alice from September 1940, the railway became busier than at any other time in its history, running four trains a day. With peace, it was only a matter of time before the political will to finish the dream of early settlers in South Australia was realized, and the railway completed to Darwin. But with the pressure to standardize the track gauge across Australia, it was first necessary to replace the old Ghan route with a standard-gauge line to Alice. A more westerly route was chosen, and the first train from Tarcoola on the Trans-Australian railway rolled into Alice Springs in October 1980. The last train over the old line ran before the end of the year, and its passing is commemorated by today's Old Ghan Railway Heritage Trail – itself something not to be undertaken lightly.

Left: Y class 2-6-0 No. 91 being coaled, an arduous task when done with baskets rather than crane or coaling stage.

Opposite: Relics pepper the railway's Heritage Trail, such as this NSU diesel-electric seen at Marree.

WALHALLA RAILWAY

GOLD WAS FOUND AT Walhalla in the mountains of Gippsland to the east of Melbourne in 1863, and though lobbying for a railway began a decade later, it was June 1904 before work started on building a route to Walhalla from a junction on the Melbourne–Orbost line at Moe. Unemployed men in Victoria were given the task, and the first 8 miles (12.8km) had been laid to Upper Moondarra when the engineering difficulties of the next section loomed large enough to halt work.

A contribution was demanded from landowners, and a bill enshrining the calculations was passed in the Legislative Assembly. When the measure lapsed, the Premier visited Walhalla to assess the position. Melbourne's *The Argus* reported: 'Every possible opportunity to urge the construction of the line was availed of by the townspeople. They talked railway morning, noon, and night. They turned the Premier's observations on the beauty of the scenery, the progressiveness of the town, and the prosperous condition of the mines into arguments for railway communication.' When the first eight miles had opened, the line attracted 'fat, poddy calves and stray cows as a convenient pathway to distant fields, which struck them as being greener... Much good steam and lumps of coal, to say nothing of picturesque language, were wasted on the calves.'

By the time the 26½-mile (42.6km) line opened through to Walhalla in May 1910, the gold had been largely worked out, the town's population was less than half the 1898 figure, and the miners used the new line to quit the town. The railway was also the means by which buildings and infrastructure were removed from the mines for reuse elsewhere, as well as facilitating the common Australian practice of physically moving homes – many miners used the railway to move their small wooden cottages.

It was one of four lines built to 2ft 6in (762mm) gauge by state-owned Victorian Railways, and the long construction period for a relatively short line reflects the way that costs for the work were voted in small sums, as well as the difficulty of the mountain terrain. As *The Argus* said, 'The country traversed is one of the roughest stretches that the railway engineers have had to face in this State. It passes through fine mountain scenery.' Those dramatic landscapes proved a saving grace for the railway. Right from the start, the line was popular with excursionists eager to view them – often from its impressive viaducts. So great was the demand that some trains ran with passengers standing in open bogie goods wagons. Revenue also came from the hillsides in the form of timber, and traffic from sawmills in the Erica area became a staple.

The most important structure on the line is the nationally listed Thomson River Bridge, which was built from steel and concrete recycled from other railways, and was the largest structure on Victoria's four narrow-gauge lines. The 100m (328ft) girder bridge comprised four concrete piers, five timber trestle piers and two timber abutment piers for the approach spans, which used wrought-iron beams from another line. Two of the river trestles supported a mild steel lattice girder span which had been used as a bridge at Tocumwal in New South Wales. Besides spectacular stretches of line cut

Opposite: The rudimentary construction of the viaduct is evident in this picture of a well-dressed outing, hauled by what is probably a contractor's locomotive.

Left: The way the railway had to be cut into the hillside is apparent in this 1906 shot of a NA 2-6-2T on a mixed freight.

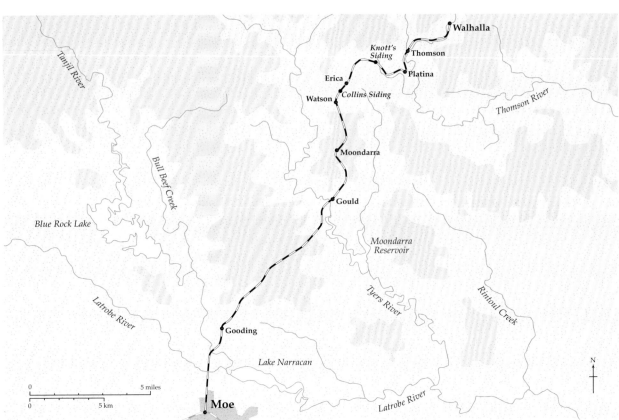

Above: One of the 17 Baldwin-designed NA class 2-6-2Ts on a mineral train in the 1910s. Two were manufactured as kits in Philadelphia and the rest assembled at Newport Workshops in Victoria.

into the steep hillside above the Thomson River, a series of trestles was built along Stringers Creek Gorge on the approach to Walhalla where the hillside was too steep to allow a foothold for the railway.

Anyone lucky enough to have visited the line before 1949 would have been able to see the unique sight of a 2ft 6in gauge Climax geared steam locomotive at work on the Tyers Valley Tramway, which went off from the Walhalla branch at Collins Siding. Not only was it the sole Climax built to that gauge, it was also the last one ever made before the Pennsylvania company ceased production in 1928. Many logging lines in North America relied on Shay and Climax locomotives to extricate trees from the forest, thanks to their ability to climb steep gradients and their tolerance of indifferent track and sharp curves. This is achieved through the drive on a Climax being transmitted to the wheels by a complex sequence of rotating shafts, universal joints and skew

bevel gears (Shays use bevel gears). Both the four-wheel bogies on a Climax are powered. When the tramway closed in 1949, the 25 ton Climax moved to a mill at Erica before being rescued by the Puffing Billy Preservation Society for occasional use on its eponymous railway near Melbourne.

Timber traffic must have been sufficiently heavy to justify use of the largest locomotive to work on the line: G42 was one of a pair of 2-6-0+0-6-2 Garratts built in 1926 by Beyer, Peacock of Manchester for Victorian Railways (the other went to the Colac–Crowes line). Probably the most powerful locomotives ever built for the 2ft 6in gauge, they were united after closure of the Walhalla line in 1955, when G42 joined G41 at Colac before that railway closed in 1962. G41 was scrapped at Melbourne's Newport Workshops, but G42 was bought for the Puffing Billy Railway and still operates some services.

By the Second World War, the population of Walhalla had shrunk to under 200, so it can have been no surprise when the Platina–Walhalla section closed in 1944. The tradition of moving buildings continued when Walhalla's station building was shifted to the suburban Melbourne station of Hartwell. The rest of the line was closed in

1952–4, and the track lifted by 1960; but proposals to demolish the Thomson River Bridge as a training exercise for the army were met by a successful public protest. Various attempts were made to revive the line, but none came to fruition until the Walhalla Railway Taskforce was formed in 1991. It was faced with a trackbed covered in blackberries and scrub, but restoration was begun by setting up a base on the site of Thomson station and working towards Walhalla. The Thomson River Bridge was reached in 1994, and its refurbishment to the original plans entailed parts being dismantled and reconditioned off-site. Once the last six bridges before Walhalla had been refettled, services began over the northernmost 2½ miles (4km) of the branch in 2002.

Bushfires in December 2006 destroyed a three-span trestle, but the Victorian State Government came to the rescue with A$195,000 of funding to rebuild the bridge and allow services to resume the following April. It is hoped to extend the line southwards to Erica.

Opposite above: The first train to Walhalla on 15 March 1910, with a long leat to power a mine waterwheel above the train.

Opposite below: The first NA, No. 1, of 1898, photographed *c.*1912. No. 1 was also the first to be scrapped, in March 1929.

Below: A packed excursion train above the Thompson River, *c.*1910. The boys on the right must have thought they had the best seats.

OTAGO CENTRAL RAILWAY

THE OTAGO CENTRAL RAILWAY (OCR) has become far better known since it shut down than it ever was during its working life, because the closed section between Middlemarch and Clyde has become one of the country's foremost bike routes. Its most southerly section between the junction with the South Island Main Trunk at Wingatui and Middlemarch is today the spectacular 64km (40-mile) Taieri Gorge Railway.

The railway was proposed to link the Central Otago settlements created by the goldrush that was more or less over by 1870. Seven routes into the Otago were surveyed and vigorously debated before work began on the victor in 1879, but it took 12 years to build just 37km (23 miles) to reach Middlemarch. This first section featured some of the longest tunnels and most challenging viaducts on the line, and was built with the help of Chinese labourers made redundant from the gold diggings. The railway became known as 'the Bridge Line' for the number and variety of bridge types, the largest being the eight-span 197.5m (648ft) Wingatui Viaduct, which was said to be the biggest viaduct in Australasia when opened by the Premier in 1887. So impressive was the scenery through the gorge that excursion trains began running immediately, though many visitors were also attracted by the engineering prowess of the line.

With the most difficult work done, it was hoped progress would be more rapid, but it proved to be so slow that critics accused the works of being little more than a soup kitchen for the unemployed. Substantial

viaducts, deep rock cuttings and more tunnels had to be built at various points where the railway changed river valleys; these were undertaken by contractors, whereas the formation of the line was done under a system of co-operative works in which each man was his own master. Groups of about a dozen workers were formed to undertake and be paid for a specific assignment. Despite periodic deputations to government and protests in newsprint and pamphlets, the remaining sections opened at a leisurely rate, reaching Clyde in 1907 and Cromwell, 236km (147½ miles) from Wingatui, in 1921.

Early travellers in winter may have had mixed feelings about a journey over the line. Any pleasure they may have taken in the varied landscapes of river gorges and upland plateaux offering panoramic views to distant ranges must have been offset by the cold and biting winds of the Otago. Until coaches with steam heating were introduced in 1928, passengers had to make do with sodium acetate foot-warmers – when these hadn't been chucked into a river by bored schoolchildren. The daily trains from each end of the line made short stops for refreshments at Hindon and Omakau; and there was a longer one for lunch at Ranfurly (previously at Hyde), while trains crossed, crews changed over and the locomotives were serviced. Representatives of Ranfurly's hotel and two private dining-rooms would meet the train with handbells to attract custom.

The Hindon refreshment room was originally run by the widow of a construction worker with nine children. Cromwell-bound trains would whistle before entering Ross Tunnel to give her the signal to start pouring the tea; advance warning of Dunedin-bound trains was given by the dog of a member of the station staff who barked as soon it heard the sound of a train rattling over 3 O'Clock

Opposite: A mixed train from Dunedin entering Middlemarch station in February 1911. Both the station and goods shed survive at the southern end of the Otago Central Rail Trail.

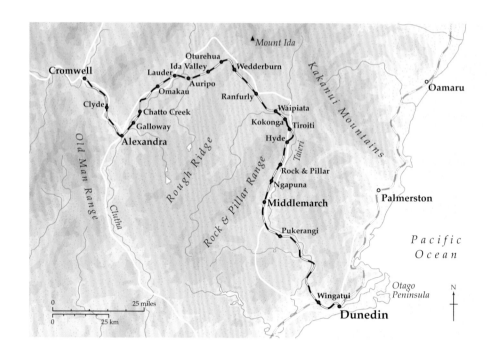

Below: A R class 0-6-4T Single Fairlie poses on Christmas Creek bridge with a Dunedin-bound train, *c.*1890. The 18 Rs were built by the Avonside Engine Co. of Bristol.

Gulch Bridge. A billy can and something to eat would be handed to the crew as their locomotive slowed past the refreshment room. Stops were also made at the lineside for the children of platelayers living in isolated places, though some were taken to school by platelayers' trolley.

Night-time running was avoided whenever possible in the early years because of the risk of rockfalls, though the danger diminished with the decline in rabbits and establishment of lineside vegetation. (Rabbits provided traffic for the railway, carried on special racks in open wagons; as many as 13,000 might be dispatched from Ranfurly in a single day.) Washouts still occurred, notably in 1980 when there were 50 slips between Wingatui and Hindon alone. Snow and ice occasionally closed the line, and in steam days, lineside fires were begun by sparks in the drier months.

The Otago Central was built to help the economic development of the region – and in carrying its staple traffics of oats and chaff for the horses of Dunedin, fruit, timber, cattle, wool and sheep (as many as 119,736 from Omakau in 1962), it fulfilled expectations. More unusual traffic included pottery clay from Hyde. The railway reduced costs of equipment and fertilizers for farmers and generated enough traffic for two goods trains a day each way, with additional workings during the fruit and stock season (January to April/May). With the deregulation of transport, traffic declined, though construction of the Clyde Dam in 1982–93 brought new flows of cement and steel. The dam flooded part of the line to Cromwell, so Clyde became the new terminus in 1980.

Diesel railcars were introduced in 1956, reducing the journey time from eight hours to a little over five, and the last regular steam train over the line ran in 1968. Excursion trains taking advantage of the line's scenic attractions became increasingly popular after the Second World War. When New Zealand Railways (NZR) decided to stop running excursion trains in 1976, the NZ Railway and Locomotive Society bought veteran carriages and hired NZR locomotives to haul them, usually as far as Pukerangi. The Society formed the Otago Excursion

Train Trust to operate them, and developed evening trains on which a four-course dinner was served during a leisurely journey through the Taieri Gorge.

A daily service was inaugurated in February 1987, using a rake of new coaches with large windows, air conditioning and catering facilities. Echoing the reliance of today's TranzAlpine trains on cruise passengers from Port Lyttelton near Christchurch, 'Cruise Ship Trains' became important on the Otago Central during the 1990s. Their success was a major factor in the Dunedin City Council taking an option to buy the line as far as Middlemarch when, in December 1989, NZR announced that it would close on 30 April 1990. However, the council called on the community to raise $1 million to fund it; within seven months $1.2 million had been raised, and the line from the Taieri Industrial Estate (4km from Wingatui) to Middlemarch was sub-leased to the Otago Excursion Train Trust following the last train from Clyde.

In common with all long-distance railway lines serving rural communities, the 149 staff (in 1950) employed in various capacities along the line formed a large community, along with their families. Economies to reduce costs gradually reduced staff numbers to less than 20, and it was rural depopulation that prompted a few visionary local people to propose converting the railway between Middlemarch and Clyde into a route primarily for cyclists.

A trust to help with fundraising and promotion was set up by the enlightened Department of Conservation, which bought the line, and it was reopened in stages, with full opening of the Otago Central Rail Trail in 2000. Bridges were re-decked and fitted with handrails, lineside toilets installed, replica gangers' huts built as shelters with information boards, and the trackbed resurfaced. The 150km (93¾-mile) Trail has become second only to farming in the local economy, attracting about 15,000 a year to complete the whole trail in addition to those on shorter rides. It has been a lifeline for B&Bs, restaurants, cafés, local museums and shops. Railway structures and memorabilia have been left intact or reinstated, and there is a display and film about the railway at the Visitor Centre in Ranfurly station.

Left: Cyclists cross Manuherekia No 1 Bridge in Poolburn Gorge. The Otago Central Rail Trail has become the most popular of New Zealand's long-distance cycle routes, attracting over 12,000 visitors a year and the largest revenue generator in the local economy after farming.

Right: The Muttontown Gully trestle crosses the Waikerikeri Stream between Alexandra and Clyde.

Below: Otago Central trains left from perhaps New Zealand's grandest station, Dunedin. Designed by the Edinburgh-trained architect and engineer George Troup, the Flemish renaissance-style building was completed in 1904. Its patterned booking-hall floor of almost 750,000 Minton tiles incorporates a locomotive.

RIMUTAKA INCLINE

UNTIL OCTOBER 1955, one of the most exciting and noisy sections of railway anywhere in the world lay in the Rimutaka Range of New Zealand's North Island. Running parallel with the east coast, the mountains posed a challenge to the builders of the 3ft 6in- (1067mm-) gauge railway from Wellington through the fertile Wairarapa Valley to Masterton. The surveyor John Rochfort spent months tramping up hill and down dale trying to find a route, and it was eventually decided that a short, very steep section of railway at a gradient of 1 in 15 on the eastern flank was preferable to a much longer route at 1 in 40, which would still have required banking assistance. The grade on the western side was a long stretch of 1 in 35.

The system chosen to enable trains to climb the 1 in 15 incline had been devised by John Barraclough Fell, a civil and mechanical engineer who cut his teeth on railway and steamship projects in the Lake District before building railways in Italy. It was to conquer the Mont Cenis Pass that he developed the system of a centre rail engaged by horizontal wheels driven by the locomotive. The centre rail was double-headed and laid on its side. The principle was not new; it had been devised by John Ericsson and Charles Blacker Vignoles in the 1830s, but not exploited.

Fell's successful application of it, to create the world's first mountain railway and link France and Italy, convinced the New Zealand government of its suitability for the Wairarapa Line. The construction contract was divided between John Brogden & Co. of London and local firms, two of the contracts covering the Rimutaka Incline: the Summit contract and the Incline contract. The former was for Summit Tunnel and the excavation of enough hillside to create a station and yard with a turntable and five houses for railway staff. Summit became one of the most isolated railway settlements anywhere.

The other contract covered the 1 in 15 incline, two other tunnels, and a station, yard and runaway siding at Cross Creek. The line opened on 16 October 1878 and for the next 77 years the H class Fell locomotives filled the valley with sound and fury as up to five locomotives on each train battled their way up the mountain. It was a spectacle few got to watch given the remoteness of the country, and passengers' appreciation of the forested slopes must have been offset by their dislike of the protracted journey time imposed by the method of working.

At first, train weights were limited by the capacity of a single locomotive: the 36-ton engine could haul 65 tons up the hill. Double heading appears to have been tried, but from 1887 up to three locomotives were carefully spaced through a train to ease the drawbar strain. This entailed a time-consuming marshalling operation at each end, though it was reduced to a commendable average of 15 minutes. The 3-mile (4.8km) climb took 40 minutes. Descending trains were retarded by Fell brake vans with a manually operated brake that pressed on the centre rail. It was unusual for a brake-van shoe to last three descents; normally they managed just one. Sometimes the weight of the descending train called for two vans, adding to the weight and reducing the revenue of the next ascending train. With the fitting of Westinghouse continuous brakes in 1903, train weights

Opposite: The Royal Train carrying the Duke of Gloucester and his party climbing the Rimutaka Incline, just above Cross Creek, January 1935. Five Fell locomotives hauled the train on the ascent to Summit.

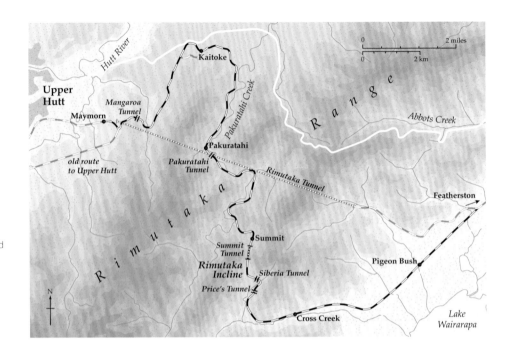

Below: No. 201 heads a packed train with four locomotives. Built in 1878, No. 201 was originally named *Mount Egmont* and was scrapped at Silverstream in 1957.

allowed five locomotives per train. Points from the incline at Cross Creek were set into the runaway siding until the signalman heard a long whistle from the leading locomotive to indicate that the train was under control.

The operating cost of the section can be imagined: a maximum permitted train weight of 260 tons required·five drivers, five firemen, a train guard and four brake-van guards. The operating conditions for the locomotive crews were none too pleasant. The 0-4-2 tank engines' outside cylinders powered the rear pair of coupled wheels and the inside cylinders rotated four horizontal driving wheels between the frames which gripped the centre rail. Because the horizontal wheels maintained their grip on the centre rail through springs rather than the cogs of a rack system, it was possible for either unit to slip, and in the noise of a tunnel it was often impossible for the crew to tell which unit had lost traction. Continuous firing was required, and the exhaust soon filled the tunnel, making conditions progressively worse for the crews of the next locomotive in the train.

Traffic grew, especially as the line was extended to reach Woodville Junction on the Palmerston North–Gisborne railway in 1897. Facilities at both Cross Creek and Summit were enlarged, the former gaining a new four-road engine shed in 1899 and a workshop that could handle all but major overhauls. Petrol and later diesel railcars nicknamed 'tin hares' were introduced for passenger services in 1936. Steam power was limited to 6mph (9.7km/h) on the ascent, but the railcars could manage 12–15mph (19–24km/h), and were much quicker on the flatter sections.

Though the Wairarapa Line was a secondary route, eventually linking Wellington with the junction of Woodville on the Palmerston North–Napier line, it was traversed by four royal trains, the last for Queen Elizabeth II and the Duke of Edinburgh in 1954.

Construction of a tunnel to cut out the incline had been proposed long before the Second World War delayed a start. Work on the 5½-mile (8.8km) Rimutaka Tunnel finally began in 1949 and was completed in 1955, the new line opening on 3 November 1955, five days after closure of the incline. Five of the Neilson- and Avonside-built locomotives were scrapped, but one was plinthed in Featherston and is now in the town's Fell Locomotive Museum – along with a Fell brake van and other exhibits and films about this remarkable railway.

Fascination with the incline, coupled with the beauty of the landscape on both approaches to the summit tunnels, encouraged the creation of the Rimutaka Rail Trail as a walking and cycling route between Maymorn and Cross Creek, which opened in 1987. Information boards pepper the route, shelters have been erected at Summit and Cross Creek, and there are remains of locomotive boilers at Summit. The ability of the tui bird to mimic sounds has led to many cyclists looking over their shoulder on the descents, thinking the sound of squealing brakes was a cyclist on their tail.

Left: A painting of the incline by Surrey-born Charles Decimus Barraud (1822–97), an amateur artist who was a chemist in Wellington, NZ.

THE AMERICAS

PASSAGE TO PATAGONIA

ANYONE TAKING THE 251-mile (402km) line from Ingeniero Jacobacci to Esquel would have found it easy to understand why Robert Leroy Parker and Harry Longabaugh – better known as Butch Cassidy and the Sundance Kid – chose the area to hole up in when on the run from Pinkerton agents over 100 years ago. The railway was built through a landscape of rugged hills the colour of bleached sand with a backdrop of snow-covered mountains, some of them extinct volcanoes. The pale earth is barren but for scattered thorn bushes and patches of coarse grass. For mile after mile not a single habitation can be seen, nor any sign of life but the occasional crumbling remains of a broken cart or the hint of a track through the scrub. It is cold for most of the year, and snow-covered during winter. The wind can tear across the land with such ferocity that trains were derailed, recalling the injunction in some narrow-gauge Indian trains that windows should be opened during high winds.

With the wind comes dust. When the novelist and travel writer Paul Theroux arrived at Ingeniero Jacobacci at two in the morning, he encountered what he described as 'no ordinary dust storm, more like a disaster in a mine shaft'. This is a Spartan land of wide-open spaces, and people have to be escaping something, needy or plain unlucky to live there. The famous bank robbers were not alone in choosing the area for its desolation. Not long before them, 153 Welsh settlers had landed from a brig to escape English oppression in banning their language from schools. They founded settlements with names

such as Trevelin and Port Madryn (after the Gwynedd estate of Sir Love Jones-Parry whose report on Patagonia encouraged the emigration from Wales), and tried to eke a living out of the land with sheep imported from the Falkland Islands. Their Welsh-speaking descendants are still there.

So the existence of a railway through such a land is a puzzle in itself. Like most of the few railways in Patagonia, the 2ft 6in (75cm) gauge line was built by Ferrocarril Patagónico to encourage the development of marginal agricultural land. It was begun in 1922, but by 1929 only 25 miles (40km) had been completed. Work was abandoned, and two years later floods destroyed much of what had been accomplished. An injection of government funds allowed work to restart in 1932, with the first section opening from Ingeniero Jacobacci to Aguada Troncoso in 1936, but it was not until 1945 that the line opened through to Esquel. By that time, as rough roads had been built, the railway never had a monopoly of what little traffic was on offer – so little that for many years there was no more than one train a week in each direction.

Today Esquel is a ski resort, though no one arrives by train; everyone flies in from Buenos Aires. For some years the more adventurous of the skiers gave up a day on the slopes for something infinitely more memorable than the twenty-seventh downhill run of the week. They helped to stave off the execution of the railway for some years, and it became part of the region's tourist infrastructure as 'La Trochita' ('little gauge'), but the struggle to maintain the steam locomotives in serviceable order, as well as a mounting deficit, eventually put paid to one of Patagonia's greatest assets – one that had been declared a National Historic Monument as recently as 1999.

Opposite: Baldwin 2-8-2 No. 3 of 1922 crosses a bridge over the Rio Chico. The total of 80 steam locomotives far exceeded the railway's traffic requirements.

The bleak single-platform station at Esquel overlooks the town of 32,000 people, founded as an offshoot of the Welsh colony of Chubut. To the north-west of Esquel is Cholila, the 4,856ha (12,000-acre) ranch which Parker and Longabaugh bought and ran between 1901 and 1907 before selling up in a hurry and moving on. No one has ever been able to prove what became of the two robbers, but the violent shoot-out in a small Bolivian town that ends the film about their notorious careers is almost certainly fiction.

The trains that left Esquel were as Spartan as the country through which they passed. The seats were hard, the windows merely filtered the dust, and a passenger-stoked wood stove was the only source of heat. It also served to boil an enamel kettle for *maté*, a herbal tea to which the locals are addicted. Long ago, some trains even had a restaurant car, but copious amounts of Argentinian wine were needed to soften the leathery steaks – even

though the country produces excellent meat, the best cuts never ended up on this railway. On another occasion the dining car caught fire after wind had derailed the train. Apart from the few tourists, the trains carried local people, many of them Araucanian Indians who lived at isolated settlements along the line.

The original locomotive fleet was built for several Patagonian narrow-gauge lines, made up of 50 2-8-2s from Henschel in Germany and another 25 2-8-2s of a different design from Baldwin in Philadelphia. All were delivered in 1922–3. In the final years, age hung heavily on the few still operable; they were limited in their speed as much by leaking steam pipes as dodgy track. Theroux likened them to 'a demented samovar on wheels'.

The climb into the *cordillera* began from the end of Esquel's platform and continued for the first 50 miles (80km). The best and most exciting vantage point was the end open balcony of a carriage, taking in the unobstructed

Above: Class 75B 2-8-2 No. 5, built by Baldwin in 1922, beneath a mesa in the barren landscape between Ingeniero Jacobacci and Manuel Choiqué.

Left: The first train enters the town on 25 May 1945, 24 years after hearing they were to become part of Argentina's railway network.

view and the scale of the mountains and hills through which the railway wound its circuitous course. A stand of poplars would herald a water stop for the locomotive, the trees providing a windbreak for the few timber shacks built of railway sleepers and caulked with mud to keep out the wind. The red-roofed huts were home to the few railway workers who maintained the track. Everyone would turn out for the train, especially when the service was down to one a week, to exchange gossip and parcels while the fireman replenished the water tanks.

The engine crew sometimes behaved as though they were driving a crack express, swinging the water hose aside, blowing the whistle and starting off with an alacrity that had unwary passengers who had been stretching their legs having to run beside the carriages to clamber aboard. The stations weren't somewhere to wait a week for the next train. Patagonian landscape has a Marmite quality: those with a love of emptiness and relatively untouched nature relish the sense of space and freedom; others see it as a barren wilderness alien to the human soul.

Even when operating efficiently, the Old Patagonian Express of Theroux's travels took 14 hours for the journey, but derailment or a locomotive failure could extend that to 24, the passengers lying in the grass waiting for rescue. On one occasion the train crew commandeered a track-gang trolley and simply abandoned the train and its passengers to their fate and a long wait for assistance. Travel on 'La Trochita' was never for the faint-hearted.

Opposite: The sparsely upholstered interior of a 1922 coach, which featured a wood-burning furnace that could be used to keep warm, for light cooking and to prepare maté tea.

Above: The utter desolation and emptiness of the landscape is writ large in this shot of Baldwin 2-8-2 No. 5 on a mixed train on 2 November 1981.

FERROCARRIL TRANSANDINO

NO CHAIN OF MOUNTAINS can rival the Andes for spectacular railways. Happily, some are still operational, despite the costs and challenges of climate and geology that go with mountain climbing of any kind. Perhaps the most regrettable closure is the first rail link between Chile and Argentina, forged through such difficult terrain that it was built to metre gauge (3ft 3⅜in), despite connecting with broad-gauge lines at each end. The line between Mendoza in Argentina and Santa Rosa de Los Andes, usually referred to as 'Los Andes', was built through the Uspallata Pass which Darwin had traversed in 1835. The commercial attraction was traffic between west and east coast ports that would replace the perils of Cape Horn; though the rail journey between Buenos Aires and Valparaíso would take about 38 hours, a sea voyage between them took 11 days.

In Chile a broad-gauge branch off the Santiago–Valparaíso line opened to Los Andes in 1874, and an indirect broad-gauge line from Buenos Aires had reached Mendoza in 1885. Construction of the 156¼-mile (250km) Ferrocarril Transandino (Transandean Railway) began on the Argentine side in 1887 and in Chile two years later, but political turmoil in both countries caused a 12-year slowing or complete cessation of work from 1891. Its resumption in 1903 was marked by a banquet in London, since this symbolized an ending of the credit restrictions which had paralyzed investment in Argentina and Chile.

Opposite: Workmen at the entrance to the summit tunnel on the Argentine side of the Transandine Railway c.1905.

Right: The length of this bridge in Aconcagua National Park gives an idea of the torrents that Andean rivers could become.

The greatest challenge was the 3,463½-yd (3,167m) summit (Cumbre) tunnel which marked the border between the two countries. The workings on the Chilean side had to be supplied by mule, and were cut off by snow for three to four months of the winter. Workers had to rely on stores built up before they were marooned. In building the railway the engineers had considered the challenge of snow, avoiding cuttings and placing their faith in the ferocious winds of the *cordillera* to blow it off the exposed track. Snowfall over a typical winter reached 21ft (6.4m), less than half the depth faced by the Canadian Pacific Railway, but the danger came from avalanches. As a consequence, sheds to protect against

these had to be built at vulnerable points; their number increased with each winter's bitter experience.

The Argentinean engineers had to find a way that would allow the railway to live alongside the River Mendoza, which it was to follow for 65 miles (104km), partly through a gorge. Like all Andean watercourses, the river was liable to huge fluctuations in flow, often within minutes of a cloudburst. The only solution was to blast a shelf for the railway high above the river. Moreover, 10 bridges had to built across the river in just 19 miles (30km). Bridge spans often had to be increased as engineers understood the river better, and to save scarce timber one bridge span was erected on earth fill during the dry season, allowing the floodwaters to sweep away the soil, leaving the completed bridge.

Though the Cumbre tunnel was the longest, another 35 tunnels had to be bored. In 1910 the simultaneous borings of the summit tunnel met, the centre lines being just 2¾in (7cm) out. Its alignment was designed to use the prevailing wind to provide ventilation and reduce the build-up of smoke. With the tunnel complete, the railway opened for public services in April 1910.

The gradients to the summit tunnel at 10,400ft (3,170m) called for the use of a central rack on both approaches, and a three-bar Abt rack was chosen – despite Dr Carl Roman Abt, the Swiss engineer who gave his name to the system, disowning the third bar in favour of just two. On the Chilean side, there were six rack sections with a ruling gradient of 1 in 12½, and in Argentina seven sections with a ruling gradient of 1 in 16.

The first rack locomotives, 2-6-2 tanks from Borsig of Berlin, soon proved inadequate, and consulting engineers were called in to design something more powerful. Dr Abt declared the task impossible, but was proved wrong by two extraordinary Kitson-Meyer 0-8-6-0 tanks built in Leeds, followed by a similar 0-6-8-0T from Esslingen in Baden-Württemberg. On both types one bogie was equipped for rack working, the other for adhesion. The cost of maintaining these complex machines encouraged electrification on the more difficult Chilean side, including the Cumbre tunnel. Wiring work began in 1927 but it was not completed until 1942, when three engines supplied from the world's leading builders of electric railway locomotives, the Swiss companies SLM and Brown Boveri, ended the cacophony of rack locomotives in the summit tunnel.

In Argentina, six- and eight-coupled tank engines proved adequate for the section from Mendoza into the foothills at Zanjón Amarillo – the rack began before the next station at Punta de Vacas. In the hope of reducing consumption of Welsh coal on heavier trains, four Manchester-built 2-6-2+2-6-2 Beyer-Garratts arrived in 1929. On the rack sections, service trains were always hauled, rather then pushed, by locomotives working bunker first to ameliorate conditions for the crew and reduce the amount of ash and cinders reaching moving parts. Propelling the deliberately light carriages into snow would not have had a happy outcome.

The crack train was the 'Pullman' international which left Mendoza westbound at 7.30am, and eastbound from Los Andes at 9.50am, usually with three chair cars, a dining- and a kitchen-car, and a baggage van, all in varnished teak. The *Locomotive* magazine of 1925 reported that 'each Pullman car consists of a large main saloon provided with 10 wicker chairs upholstered in green leather and a couch at each end of the saloon, also a small private compartment for six persons and a lavatory... The whole of the interior is of a special selected mahogany, while the metallic fittings are of oxidized silver finish. The dining-car is an open saloon with two semi-cross partitions...' It took a little over 12

Above right: The rack locomotives on the Transandino were fitted with three-bar Abt rack. Three of the Kitson-Meyers have survived.

Right: The station at Cacheuta in the foothills of the Andes on the Argentinian side, *c.*1920. Natural hot springs made it a spa town.

hours to cover the 156¼ miles (250km) to Los Andes, but the mountain landscapes would have kept most first-time passengers enthralled. However, daylight runs were made not for their aesthetic enjoyment, but to avoid the need to convey sleeping cars with such a poor ratio of tare weight to payload.

Even though the railway was under a single administrative organization from 1923, discord grew to a point where all traffic was suspended for much of 1932. Two years later, flood damage between Punta da Vacas and Mendoza was so severe that the railway on the Argentine side remained closed until the exigencies of war prompted the Argentine government to take over the line in 1939 and put repairs in hand. It reopened in 1944.

Containerization helped to compensate for the costs of the break of gauge at either end, and the small passenger traffic was taken over by single railcars and Hungarian three-car diesel units. Tension between the two countries in 1977–8 caused another suspension of services, during which road vehicles used the Cumbre tunnel on an alternate one-way basis. Though train operations resumed, the passenger service ended in 1979 and the last freight ran in 1984. There have been desultory efforts to reopen the line, with occasional reports of token efforts at repairs. Though its resurrection would revive one of the world's most spectacular journeys, the high cost makes it improbable.

Below: Abandoned railway buildings at Las Cuevas on the Argentinian side of the summit tunnel. Operating staff on the trans-Andean railways required stoicism to see them through the winters.

ferro Carril Trasandino   Valparaiso 28 de Julio de 1908

Left: One of the two Borsig 2-6-2 rack tanks employing Joy valve gear which were delivered from Berlin in 1905. A rack engine was fitted between the first and second coupled axles.

Below: One of the Chilean Transandino 1-C-C-1 rack/adhesion locomotives supplied by SLM/Brown Boveri in Switzerland. The six motors were supplied with 3000V DC.

MADEIRA–MAMORÉ RAILWAY

FEW RAILWAYS HAVE such an exotic and tragic story as this 224-mile (358km) railway in the heart of Amazonia which gained the sobriquet of 'Devil's Railroad' for the hardships and fatalities that afflicted its builders. It has a parallel in the history of the Panama Canal, since both first attempts were seared by a shocking death toll and had to be abandoned when the money ran out.

The origin of the metre-gauge (3ft 3⅜in) Madeira–Mamoré Railway can be said to have been an accident that took place in Boston, Massachusetts in 1839 when Charles Goodyear dropped a mixture of rubber and sulphur on to a hot stove and discovered the process that became known as vulcanization. Previously the utility of rubber had been limited by its reaction to heat, which rendered it sticky, and cold, which made it brittle. As a consequence of Goodyear's fluke, the production of wild rubber in Brazil soared and was given even greater impetus by the invention of the pneumatic tyre and the explosive demand for bicycles and automobiles. The huge value of the commodity prompted Andrew Carnegie's rueful comment, 'I should have chosen rubber'.

At the height of the rubber boom, 5,000 men a week were venturing up the Amazon to its centre at Manaus, hoping to share in the wealth that made the burgeoning city the highest per capita consumer of diamonds in the world. The three species of wild *Hevea*

that produced the latex covered two million square miles of tropical rainforest. The challenge was finding them. Exemplifying nature's genius, trees seldom grew close to one another to reduce the chance of contracting South American leaf blight, but this made the process of extracting latex more labour-intensive. The rubber barons became notorious for their cruel exploitation of peasants and Indians.

Given difficulties over Bolivian access to the Pacific, a train service that gave the country access to the Amazon would allow it to export its rubber to Europe. The railway was a means of circumventing the 19 rapids and cataracts of the River Madeira which made navigation nearly impossible over a stretch of 200 miles (320km).

The railway would link Porto Velho on the eastern bank of the River Madeira, a tributary of the Amazon, with Guajará-Mirim on the border with Bolivia. Though railway engineers had created many astounding feats of engineering by the 1860s, no one had yet built a railway through such impenetrable rainforest. In 1867 the Bolivian government commissioned a former US Union army officer, Colonel George Earl Church, to construct the railway. He wasted no time, raising money in Europe and beginning construction from Porto Velho, 1,650 miles (2,640km) from the Atlantic.

The logistics alone were daunting. Supplies of provisions for the workforce and construction materials had to be transported over hundreds, often thousands of miles. The polyglot workforce came from 52 countries, including the Caribbean islands, Britain, China, Denmark, Germany, Greece, India, Portugal, Spain and

Opposite: The railway's first locomotive, Baldwin 4-4-0 No. 12 *Colonel Church* of 1878, was found buried in jungle creepers when construction resumed after 34 years. A group of officials pose in front of the revived product of Philadelphia.

the US. Some of the US workers were drawn from the 7,000 southern Confederates who had been encouraged to settle in Brazil by the Brazilian emperor Dom Pedro II.

By 1879, just 5 miles (7.5km) of line had been laid at a cost of an estimated 7,000 to 10,000 lives from dysentery, malaria, yellow fever and beriberi, insect bites, wild animal attacks, Indian raids and brawling. The supply steamer of the contractors, P. & T. Collins of Philadelphia, had sunk in a storm with the loss of about 80 lives. Since the ship was the workers' only link with civilization, the sinking left them on the edge of starvation. Unsurprisingly, investors lost confidence, and Church had to abandon the project. In an echo of the construction of the first Panama Canal, the jungle reasserted itself and gradually subsumed the workings. Apart from a brief attempt at revival by the Brazilian government in 1882–3, nothing was done until 1903 when Brazil signed an agreement with Bolivia promising to complete the railway within four years.

Another American, Percival Farquhar, was given the job of realizing the commitment, and he assembled a second 'Foreign Legion of the jungle' to build it, many of them veterans of the Panama Canal. Several hundred men were recruited from Germany, but the reality of the upper Amazon proved so different from their conception of it that few stayed. Nine of them attempted to return to the Atlantic on an improvised raft, but five of their heads were later found floating in the river, and the other four were never seen again. Germany was one of a number of countries that banned its citizens from working on the Madeira–Mamoré Railway.

Farquhar also negotiated a 69-year concession on the railway and large areas of rubber trees, but he reportedly never even visited Porto Velho, directing construction from Rio. He was a hard taskmaster, but he provided a hospital and laid down strict instructions to maintain health. About 30 work camps, 7 miles (11km) apart, were set up. Encased in 34 years of forest growth, the workers found a handsome Baldwin-built 4-4-0 of 1878, left where it had been abandoned, and managed to restore it. Meat from the jungle, beans and rice were the main diet, but oranges and grapefruit were provided to counter scurvy and other ailments. There was even an ice plant and wireless communication between Porto Velho and the camps.

Though Farquhar's precautions prevented a repetition

of the earlier death toll through mosquito bites and other causes, about 2,000 died during the second campaign and some challenges remained the same. Rain would reduce camps to quagmires, collapse tents in the middle of the night, and cause mudslides that derailed work trains. Because Brazilian wood was susceptible to termite infestation, sleepers lasted only a few months, compelling the importation of wood from Formosa and prompting the plantation of eucalyptus for locomotive fuel and sleepers; the trees' natural oil deterred termites. So it was a great achievement when the golden spike – the traditional way of marking completion of a railway with flat-bottomed rails – was driven home on 1 August 1912 at Guajará-Mirim, though services appear to have started the previous April.

However, the economic foundation of the railway was already being undermined by a process that had begun in 1876. Attempts to transport seeds and destroy the Brazilian monopoly had failed, but that year the first steamship plied the Amazon and carried a British explorer, Henry Wickham, who succeeded in bringing out 70,000 *Hevea brasiliensis* seeds. Carried as a special consignment by train from Liverpool, the seeds were taken to the Royal Botanic Garden at Kew and successfully germinated, producing 2,800 plants. Within a month, they were on a ship for Ceylon. Though it took years of experimentation, by 1907 there were 10 million rubber trees growing in plantations in Ceylon and Malaya, with production costs one-fifth of Brazil's. Moreover, Bolivia and Chile were reconciled, and the opening of the Panama Canal allowed Bolivian exports to reach the Atlantic without recourse to the Amazon. World war was the last straw for many of Farquhar's companies, and his creditors sent a court-appointed administrator, a former Governor of the Philippines, W. Cameron Forbes, to try to recover their funds.

COLONEL GEORGE EARL CHURCH (1835–1910)
AND PERCIVAL FARQUHAR (1864–1953)

George Church was born in New Bedford, Massachusetts, and gained experience of railway construction in the US and Argentina before serving in the 11th Rhode Island Infantry during the Civil War. Following a period in Mexico, he explored the Amazon, acquiring such linguistic and geographic knowledge that he was an astute appointment for the Madeira-Mamoré project. After its failure, he continued to advise on developments in South America and write about the continent. He spent the last 30 years of his life living in London, becoming a Vice-President of the Royal Geographical Society and the first non-British citizen elected to its council.

Percival Farquhar came from a wealthy Pennsylvanian Quaker family, studied engineering at Yale University and developed railway and commercial interests in the US, Cuba, Guatemala and Russia as well as Latin America. His focus was Brazil, and he became one of the foremost investors in the country between 1905 and 1918, though he went bankrupt in 1914. He rebuilt his business empire, only to fall again after the 1929 crash when he finally left Brazil. He died in New York City where he had been a member of the State Assembly. Questions over his business methods and morality make him a controversial figure in the country's history.

Though revenue on the railway peaked as early as 1913 and declined thereafter, it continued to operate. After the 1929 economic crash the Brazilian government took over the railway, leading to years of litigation until the 1909 agreement was rescinded in 1937. The railway had a swan-song during the Second World War when US warships sailed up the Amazon to Porto Velho to take on consignments of rubber delivered by the railway. The train service in the final decades was a weekly railcar which took 12 hours, and a twice-weekly steam-hauled train with an overnight stop at Abunã. It finally closed on 1 July 1971 and much of it was dismantled within a few years.

In 1991 the state of Rondônia appealed to descendants of the railway to help resurrect a section. One of the Philadelphia-built locomotives survives in Mutum-Paraná. The railway was featured in a 2005 TV mini series *Mad Maria* and one of the locomotives used is at Guajará-Murim where there is a railway muscum. A 7km section has been preserved at Porto Velho, part funded by the energy company building the Santo Antonio Dam, whose construction will submerge much of the trackbed.

Opposite: Restoration of the station at Porto Velho and a section of the line began in 1991, which enabled the railway to feature in films. Baldwin Pacific No. 50 of 1925 hauls a special train.

Below: The decorated Baldwin 2-6-0 No. 7 of 1909 suggests this may have been the opening ceremony on 30 April 1912. In 2005, the railway was listed by Brazil's National Institute of Artistic and Historical Heritage.

ESTRADA DE FERRO CANTAGALO/ LEOPOLDINA RAILWAY

BRITAIN HAD INTERESTS in many of South America's railways, and the largest British enterprise in Brazil was the Leopoldina Railway, which eventually operated almost 2,000 miles (3,200km) of metre-gauge (3ft 3⅜in) lines to the north of Rio de Janeiro. Among the 38 railways which became part of the Leopoldina was the Cantagalo Railway (Estrada de Ferro Cantagalo) which was Brazil's first mountain railway and used the Fell system (see p.115). It opened on 18 December 1873 and linked the coastal plain at Niterói with Nova Friburgo, a village created in 1820 by Roman Catholic exiles from Fribourg in Switzerland, and Cantagalo. Coffee was grown in the mountainous Paraíba Valley, and its transport for export was expected to be the major source of freight traffic.

North of Rio a 300-mile (480km) mountain chain parallels the coast some 15–50 miles inland; the Serra do Mar presented a formidable barrier to railway builders, with many rounded and barren summits like the Sugar Loaf of Rio, others wreathed in thick vegetation. A turning point in construction of railways to export coffee grown in the region was a law passed in 1852 which guaranteed a 5 per cent return to investors in an approved line. Some provinces made a contribution to increase this to 7 per cent.

Opposite: This 2-6-0 was one of a class of 15 engines built for Brazil's metre gauge Leopoldina Railway in 1899/1900. The engine was a woodburner and worked at the Usina Santamaria in Brazil's Campus state having been pensioned off from main line service.

Unusually, construction of what became part of the Cantagalo Railway began in the middle with a 5ft 3in (1600mm) gauge line from Porto das Caixas to Cachoeiras de Macacu, opening in 1860. This was extended in 1866 towards Niterói at Vila Nova/Itambí where there was a ferry terminal for Niterói. Work on the next part between Cachoeiras and Nova Friburgo started in March 1870. To begin with, the maximum gradient was 1 in 30, but from Boca do Mato ('mouth of the forest') to Teodoro de Oliveira it steepened to a maximum of 1 in 12½ and an average of 1 in 14. The railway climbed from 728ft (222m) above sea level to 3,542ft (1,080m) in just 7⅔ miles (12.2km). From the summit at Teodoro de Oliveira, the gradients on to Nova Friburgo were easier. A rack system of some kind was required for the steepest part, and fortuitously for both parties the Fell-system Mont Cenis Railway was about to be decommissioned with the introduction of the eponymous tunnel between France and Italy, which opened in October 1871.

John Barraclough Fell (see p.115) gave a lecture to the British Association in 1870 describing the Cantagalo Railway, so agreements must already have been made to sell rails and locomotives for use in Brazil, the only exceptions being locomotives Nos 1 and 2 which went to the Lausanne–Echallens Railway in Switzerland. Use of this equipment naturally dictated the unusual gauge of 1100mm (3ft 7⁵⁄₁₆in).

Before the Cantagalo Railway opened, three new 0-4-0T locomotives were ordered from Manning Wardle of Leeds, which built them in 1872 and tested them in June on the disused incline of George Stephenson's Whitby

& Pickering Railway (now part of the North Yorkshire Moors Railway) between Beck Hole and Goathland. They were driven by the Assistant Superintendent on the Mont Cenis Railway, Thomas Morton, who had intended to go to the Cantagalo line as Locomotive Superintendent. Two of the locomotive's four cylinders powered the four carrying wheels, while the other two were 'placed vertically one above the other between the side frames' and drove the four friction wheels which revolved against the centre rail. The power of the inside cylinders was transmitted, said *The Engineer*, by 'a motion which must be seen to be understood'. Among those who witnessed the trials were James Brunlees (as consulting engineer to the São Paulo Railway and other railways in Brazil), Robert Fairlie (who invented the locomotive type that bears his name), and John Fell.

The railway between Cachoeiras and Nova Friburgo opened in 1873, and the final part between Vila Nova and Niterói in 1874. A third rail was added to the broad gauge sections in 1871 before the gauge of the lower sections was converted from 5ft 3in (1600m) to 1100m (3ft 7⁵/₁₆in) in the mid-1870s using heavier rail, which reduced the railway's revenues. In 1876 the railway had

20 locomotives for the upper sections: nine for the Fell system, a single Fairlie and 10 for the ordinary sections.

For the steepest section, trains were split into parts of not more than 40 tons either ascending or descending. Trains were subdivided at Cachoeiras to a maximum of four vehicles and locomotives changed for a Fell locomotive; they were further subdivided 4¹/₃ miles (7km) further on at Boca do Mato with no more than two vehicles behind a locomotive. At Teodoro de Oliveira trains were re-marshalled for the onward journey to Nova Friburgo and beyond. On the Fell section, there were two intermediate stations, at Penna and Registro, and descending trains had a longer wait at the former while the locomotive's central rail brake blocks were changed. A special pit was provided so that the firemen could crawl underneath the engines and replace brake blocks on descending trains. Three sets of brake shoes were normally used for each descent, and a brakesman rode on each carriage. The maximum speed was 9mph (14.4km/h) both ascending and descending.

However, the severe curves of the line, combined with the rigidity of the locomotives' horizontal drive mechanism, caused fractures, and an order was placed

with Baldwin of Philadelphia for more powerful locomotives. Astonishingly, these 0-6-0Ts proved capable of ascending the incline by adhesion alone with a payload of sorts, making it the steepest section of trunk railway to be operated by adhesion. The payload, though, was an accountant's nightmare, the 40-ton locomotives hauling a train of just 45 tons.

The central rail was used for braking only on the descent which accounted for the heaviest loads, so it is no wonder that the buffer beams were loaded with spare brake blocks. Norman Dickson was the engineer-in-chief, and experienced what happened when a train got out of control: 'He was carrying out a periodical inspection of the line from his special carriage coupled to a locomotive. In coming down the bank something went wrong, and the train got away. The engineer-in-chief admits he had an uncomfortably anxious few minutes. He felt the train gather speed, and suffered violent oscillation as the train

swung round the bends. Just as he was wondering what would be the end, there was a jump and a crash. The engine had left the track, rolled over, and his car was astride the overturned locomotive. He crawled out of the wreck, badly shaken and bruised, but otherwise little worse for his adventures, though the unfortunate driver was killed.'

Those willing to brave the shower of hot cinders raining down from the locomotive by leaning out to enjoy the spectacular mountain views could sometimes see the rail beneath the carriage, so sharp were some curves. Because trains followed one another, a sharp lookout was required in case a train had halted mid-section. Traffic in the summer was heavy with people from the coast seeking the cool of the mountain resorts, and passenger trains might have to ascend in up to seven sections. Between the passengers, goods wagons were taken up and down, so there was continuous work for

locomotives between 5am and 10pm. Entry into Nova Friburgo was spectacular, passing along the road in front of shops like the still-open street sections of the Guayaquil & Quito Railway in Ecuador or Bad Doberan in northern Germany.

In 1887 the Cantagalo Railway was acquired by the Leopoldina Railway which was busy buying more lines than it was building, but by 1897 it was in financial trouble and was taken over by a British-based company of the same name. During the 1890s the Cantagalo's gauge was narrowed to one metre (3ft 3⅜in) to conform with the rest of the Leopoldina Railway. It continued to expand until 1930, when it too got into financial difficulties. The Brazilian government took it over in 1949 and closed many of the lines.

New locomotives with steam-operated Fell centre brakes were ordered from North British Locomotive Co. of Glasgow in 1928 and again in 1944–6. Four Beyer Garratts of unusual 2-4-2+2-4-2 wheel arrangement were delivered to the Leopoldina for the Cantagalo in 1943, having dodged U-boats in the Atlantic, and they worked over the severely curved line between Portella and Cordiero with a ruling gradient of 1 in 30 uncompensated. The railway was closed in 1964 and the track on the incline lifted the following year, bringing to an end one of the most idiosyncratic railways in South America.

Above: The inauguration of the Cantagalo Railway in June 1860. Many railways went to town for the opening ceremony, with triumphal arches.

Opposite above: The summit of the rack on the Leopoldina's Rio–Petropolis line at Alto da Serra station, showing the Riggenbach rack.

Opposite below: A typical Leopoldina freight train, taken at Neves on 22 November 1919. Many locomotives were fitted with bulbous spark-arresting chimneys and huge headlamps.

ASUNCIÓN–ENCARNACIÓN

WHILE OTHER SOUTH AMERICAN countries were busy building railways in the second half of the 19th century, landlocked Paraguay was recovering from the disastrous War of the Triple Alliance in 1864–70, when it had fought Argentina, Brazil and Uruguay and lost 60–70 per cent of its male population. Planning of the 376km (235-mile) Central Paraguay Railway between the capital, Asunción, and the border with Argentina at Encarnación had begun in 1854 under the country's first prime minister, Carlos Antonio López. He opened up the country after decades of isolation following independence from Spain in 1811, and settled on the Iberian gauge of 5ft 6in (1675mm). The first section from Asunción as far as Trinidad opened in 1861, and before the end of the year it had extended for 45 miles (72km) as far as Paraguarí – and there it stopped for the next 28 years.

Carlos Antonio López's son took the country into the war and died at its conclusion. The devastation it brought prevented anything being done until 1886, when some further construction was attempted, but the following year the Paraguay Central Railway was incorporated under English law. It acquired the railway from the government and finished the uncompleted line to Villa Roca in 1889. Financial problems delayed completion to Encarnación until 1911, by which time the line had been regauged to avoid a break of gauge with the standard-gauge British-owned Argentine North Eastern Railway. All the new equipment was ordered from the UK and the regauging was completed in 1913, allowing a through

Above: The North British Locomotive Co. of Glasgow built 14 of these 2-6-0s for the Ferrocarril Presidente Carlos Antonio Lopez Railway. No. 59 is seen at San Salvador Junction.

train service between Buenos Aires and Asunción to begin on 17 October 1914 using carriages from both railways and the Entre Ríos Railway. The only other line was a branch from the main line at San Salvador to Abaí.

The landscape may have lacked the excitement of the Andes or the coastal mountains of Brazil, but the railway's locomotives and character were delightful. It also had the distinction of being almost certainly the last all-steam national railway and having a fleet of wood-burning locomotives. All but two of the handsomely proportioned 2-6-0s, 2-6-2Ts and 0-6-0Ts dated from the conversion to standard gauge and were built by the North British Locomotive Co. in Glasgow or Hawthorn

Opposite: One of the wood-burning North British-built 2-6-0s, No. 101 of 1910, heads up the main street of Encarnación. The railway took to the streets at both ends of the line.

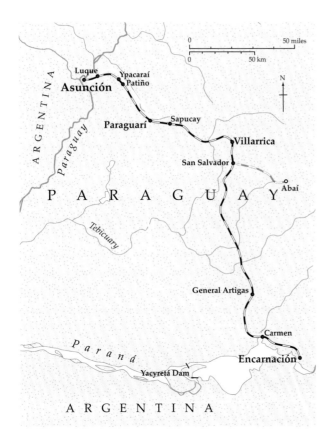

waiting firebox, the locomotive water tank replenished, a wagon attached, or warm bearings attended to. Though trains at one time had a dining-car, the state of the track made the journey from plate to mouth a rather hit and miss affair. Derailments were not uncommon.

Added interest was the link to Argentina, by train ferry across the River Paraná between Encarnación and Posadas where the Ferrocarril General Urquiza provided connections to Buenos Aires and with the Brazilian and Uruguayan railway networks. It was a performance loading the train ferry, due to the discrepancy in height between Encarnación station and the loading point. The train had to run through the streets of the town before gingerly descending a switchback to zigzag to the terminal. There, the coaches were lowered down an incline one at a time by a steam-operated winch and cable. Once the twin-track ferry boat was loaded with six carriages, it crossed the river to Posadas.

Very few visitors travelled the 50-mile (80km) Abaí branch, which had one return working a week. An intrepid traveller recalled sharing the 01.30 train with locals whose pigs, sheep and chickens were tethered to the longitudinal seats, lit by a solitary light bulb swaying

Right: The postage stamp featuring Paraguay's first locomotive, a 2-2-2T of 1861, later converted to a 4-2-2.

Leslie in Newcastle in 1910–13. Two 2-6-0s were added by the Yorkshire Engine Co. of Sheffield in 1953. A bogie wagon of logs supplemented the tender stack, and the fireworks from the chimney at night were like thousands of fireflies cavorting above the train.

An imposing station building was provided in the capital, designed in a blend of Gothic and French Renaissance styles, with a magnificent colonnade beside the street. It is now a museum of the railway, containing a 5ft 6in (1675mm) gauge 4-2-2 well tank which has featured on a Paraguayan postage stamp. Once out of the city, the line passed through flat though pleasant countryside, and the attractive if basic stations were often sheltered by luxuriant vegetation and trees. Station stops were frequently protracted as wood was passed nearer the

Left: The state of the track can be appreciated from the carriage rooflines in this picture of North British-built 2-6-0 No. 53.

Below: There was one branch line off the main line, to Abaí from San Salvador Junction. Here 2-6-0 No. 83 borrowed from Argentina is seen waiting with the train on trackwork barely visible for grass.

from the centre mounting. He stayed overnight in the nearest thing to a hotel in the village, washed at a well, and slept poorly, worried that he would oversleep and miss the 07.30 departure. He need not have worried: the stationmaster sent a boy to wake and escort him to the station, carrying his case.

In 1961, the government took over the railway and renamed it Ferrocarril Presidente Carlos Antonio López after its founder, but the loss of British administration marked the start of a long decline; prior to this change, trains took 12 hours to reach Encarnación from Asunción, but by 1968 they were scheduled to take 16 and usually took longer. The sleeping-car service with Argentina was discontinued in 1972, and the ferry ceased operation with the opening of the San Roque González de Santa Cruz road/rail bridge in 1990, though construction of a hydroelectric dam at Yacyretá had flooded part of the railway on the Argentinian side. Heavy rainfall in 1996 put an end to the surviving service between Asunción and Ypacaraí, but occasional trains and freights appeared to run.

A new 29km (18-mile) alignment was opened in 2012 by the two countries with bridges over the Zaimán, Negro and Tranquera rivers. Besides freight of largely agricultural products, a passenger service between Encarnación and Posadas was set up in 2014 with an ex-Netherlands Railways two-car diesel unit; it carried 100,000 passengers in its first month.

In recent years, freight from Argentina was brought over the bridge and transferred to lorries. There is a proposal to operate a tourist service between Luque and Aregua with a possible extension to Ypacaraí and even Sapucay, where the remarkable workshops, full of belt-driven British machine tools, have been opened as a museum. There is also a suggestion that the entire line between Asunción and Encarnación might be reinstated.

Left: The crude but serviceable ramp that linked the train ferry which shuttled between Encarnación and Posadas in Argentina before the bridge in the background was opened.

Opposite above: The railway once had 12 tank locomotives, all built by Hawthorn Leslie in Newcastle-upon-Tyne, UK. No. 2, a 2-6-2T of 1910, stands by the platform at Sapucay where the railway's workshops were a time-warp of historic tools belt-driven from overhead shafts.

Opposite below: The weekly coach to Buenos Aires from Asunción on the *Roque Saenz Pena* train ferry at Pacu-Cua.

KETTLE VALLEY RAILWAY

THE KETTLE VALLEY RAILWAY (KVR) is probably better known today than it was when it linked Hope and Midway in British Columbia. Until the closure of its final section in 1989, it was a magnet for rail buffs because of attributes that prompted the men who built it to call it 'McCulloch's Wonder', in tribute to its chief engineer; whereas today its trackbed has become one of the most popular bike routes in Canada, attracting tourists from around the world.

In common with many of the province's railways, construction of the KVR posed 'superlative difficulties' in the phrase of the country's Prime Minister Alexander Mackenzie. The line had its origin in the discovery of silver in the Kootenays, and the demand for a railway that would reduce American influence by linking them with the coast. It was also part of the decades-long strategic battle between James Hill's Great Northern Railway in the US and the Canadian Pacific Railway (CPR), which funded the KVR's construction.

The KVR's charter was granted in 1901, but it was 1910 before work began. The CPR chose the highly experienced Alexander McCulloch to build it, knowing the challenges he would face in constructing over 300 miles (480km) of railway across three mountain ranges. To keep the gradient above 1 in 45 on the climb east from Penticton to Chute Lake, a spiral tunnel and a huge loop

were required, but locomotive crews still faced 27 miles at this grade. The toughest section to build was through the Coquihalla Pass, the 38 miles between Hope and Coquihalla requiring 43 bridges, 12 tunnels and 15 snow sheds. Per mile, it cost five times the Canadian average for railway construction.

One of the line's delightful idiosyncrasies stemmed from McCulloch's love of Shakespeare; he named the stations on the Coquihalla section after prominent characters in the plays – Othello, Lear, Jessica, Portia, Iago, Romeo and Juliet – and workers recalled evenings around a fire with McCulloch reciting the Bard's words from memory.

Opposite: An eastbound train poses on West Fork Canyon Creek (now Pooley Creek) trestle in Myra Canyon on its way from Penticton to Midway, *c*.1918.

Right: The nine-span Ladner Creek Bridge in the Coquihalla Pass was set on the sharpest of the Coquihalla line's 234 curves.

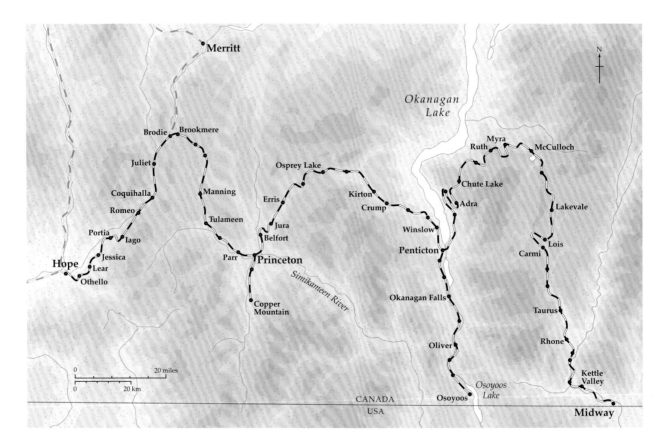

The line between Midway and Merritt, on an already built branch between Spences Bridge and Nicola, opened in 1915, and the rest of the line westward to Hope in July the following year. The First World War was not an auspicious time to open a railway, and the service was tri-weekly until 1919, when a café-observation or dining-car formed part of two expresses, named *Kootenay* and *Kettle Valley*.

It was a tough section to operate; eastbound trains faced 36 miles of 1 in 45, calling for a 'helper' locomotive, and snow closed the line for five out of the first seven winters. Brakemen were required to ride on boxcars to be able to operate the brake wheels, but there were many casualties and fatalities when a jolt caused them to lose their footing. Perhaps the most bizarre accident occurred when the trunk of a circus elephant protruded from a boxcar and dislodged a brakeman from his perch, fortunately without too serious consequences. The KVR

also had to contend with forest fires, rockfalls, landslides, washouts and even plagues of grasshoppers that made the rails so greasy that locomotives were reduced to a standstill.

For those who relished the visceral sight and sound of two or even three steam locomotives battling their way upgrade through rugged mountain landscapes, the KVR proved one of North America's foremost draws. Behind the sound of the exhaust lay the stamina of the stoker (fireman) and the skill of the engineer (driver). As brakeman Bill Presley recalled: 'Old "Ring Ass" MacKay, he could be mean at times, but he was a real good engineer. He could take you down the Coquihalla on a freight train, just like a passenger. Real good hogger. You wouldn't think he'd be working his engine, but he just had it in the right spot, coming up grade. Working the engine as it should be worked. I've seen fellows tearing an engine apart.'

Right: Penticton station housed the railway's main office and was close to the steamer wharf. 2-8-0 No. 3405 waits to leave with a passenger train.

Below: View through the Othello or Quintette tunnels in the Coquihalla Canyon, blasted for the Kettle Valley Railway between 1911 and 1916.

A journey over the line was full of scenic variety and heart-in-mouth moments from numerous dizzying drops as the train rattled across narrow trestles with not so much as a handrail. Many thought the line never more beautiful than on a moonlit night in winter, and one passenger recalled the pleasures of admiring it from a Chesterfield sofa he dragged on to the train's rear-end balcony.

Westbound trains from Midway soon joined the Kettle River and then the West Kettle River before threading Myra Canyon and the long switchback descent into Penticton. After a brush with Okanagan Lake and its CPR-owned sternwheel steamers, trains faced an equally fearsome climb to Osprey Lake where wintertime passengers might see the ice being cut into blocks for preserving the next summer's fruit crop. Dropping down to Princeton, the line followed the forested Tulameen River. Just beyond Tulameen was Otter Lake whose 1919 crop of ice blocks filled 3,000 boxcars in 15 days.

Climbing the eastern foothills of the Cascade Mountains, trains reached the divisional point and railway settlement of Brookmere, which was the base for pusher crews and snow-plough trains. After a short dip to Brodie, it was uphill again to the westernmost summit

at Coquihalla. The steep descent to Hope called for skill and care to avoid runaways, and the conductors would be heaving on the brake club to screw the brakes on as hard as they would go.

The Depression during the 1930s encouraged thoughts of abandoning the costly KVR, but the outbreak of war put paid to the idea, and by the end of the conflict the line was moving 14,000 boxcars of Okanagan fruit a year – apples, peaches, plums, pears and Cantaloupe melons. Fortunately the weaker wooden trestles had been strengthened, filled or replaced by steel. After the war the opening of the Hope-Princeton highway accelerated a relentless decline in passenger and freight traffic, and the last dining-car ran in 1957. Three serious washouts in 1959 put paid to the Coquihalla section, and the last regular passenger train over the rest of the KVR ran in 1964, the final freight in 1989.

The railway has not disappeared entirely; since 1995 a 6¼-mile (10km) section between Prairie Valley station and Canyon View Siding has given visitors the chance to gain an idea of the railway's appeal as they ride behind a 1912-built steam locomotive. For those wanting to see the rest of the line, much can be walked or cycled,

Left: One of the 19 wooden railway trestles built through Myra Canyon. Today's Kettle Valley Rail Trail and the Columbia & Western Rail Trail form the longest rail trail network in British Columbia, from Hope to Castlegar.

ALEXANDER McCULLOCH (1864–1933)

Born into a poor farming family in Lanark County, Ontario, Alexander McCulloch graduated as an accountant but sought a different life on the west coast, working in a sawmill before taking a succession of railway construction jobs. By his time on the Lake Superior & Ishpeming Railway, he had become resident engineer, and when that line was completed he walked 100 miles in three days to secure a surveying position on the CPR's Crowsnest Pass line. His professional skills were held in such high regard that the CPR and Grand Trunk Pacific Railway vied for his services. Unusually, after completing the KVR, the engineer took the position of KVR Superintendent of Operations.

thanks to restoration of 14 of the 18 trestles in the Myra Canyon section after they burned down during the 2003 Okanagan Mountain firestorm. The dramatic section through the five Quintette Tunnels (also known as the Othello Tunnels) is part of a walking trail in Coquihalla Canyon Provincial Park near Hope.

Above: CPR 2-8-0 No. 3716 was built by the Montreal locomotive Works in 1912 and after restoration featured in various feature films before moving to the Kettle Valley Steam Railway at Summerland.

CANADIAN PACIFIC:
THE BIG HILL NEAR FIELD, BC

CANADA WAS MADE by the railway. Confederation was based on promises to Nova Scotia and New Brunswick for a line linking them to Quebec and Ontario, and on a later undertaking, made to the colony of British Columbia, to provide a transcontinental railway that would persuade it to join the Canadian Confederation rather than entertain overtures from the United States. That commitment was realized by a deal between the government and the Canadian Pacific Railway (CPR): in exchange for about $25 million and 25 million acres (10 million hectares) of land, Canada would have a railway link across 2,909 miles (4,680 km) between Montreal and Vancouver.

Whole books have been devoted to the monumental feat of building the railway, which owes much to the Illinois-born William Van Horne, the CPR's general manager and vice-president who oversaw its construction. Inevitably the most difficult part was through the Rocky Mountains. Government surveys had favoured a route via the Yellowhead Pass, but the CPR preferred a more southerly course. The government responded that it would relent only on condition that the Rockies should be penetrated at least 100 miles (160km) north of the international border. This compelled the CPR to use Kicking Horse Pass, which marked the Continental Divide.

The die was cast for 4 miles (6.6km) of railway that were to be an operating nightmare, but would come to be known – along with the Semmering Pass in Austria, the Bolan Pass in India and England's Lickey Incline – as an especially exciting stretch of railway to travel over or to watch three or four steam locomotives heaving a train uphill. To adhere to the maximum gradient stipulated by the government, a tunnel would have been required through Mount Stephen. The cost aside, this would have taken years of work. The commitment made to British Columbia in 1871 to complete the line within 10 years had already been broken, due to a string of difficulties in its financing and construction. So the decision was taken to build a temporary line that would break the government-prescribed limit on gradient in spectacular fashion.

In the 10 miles (16km) between Hector and Field, the vertical difference of 1,143ft (348m) had to be overcome by what became known as 'The Big Hill', 4.1 miles (6.6km) of railway with a gradient of 1 in 22. In a portent of things to come, the first construction train to descend the newly finished track over the pass on 28 May 1884 ran away and ended up in the Kicking Horse River, killing three workmen. Talking to navvies from the site, Frederick A. Talbot was told that 'the ballast trains failed time after time to secure a grip on the metals, and with their driving-wheels spinning round madly in the forward direction they skidded backwards down-hill.'

Consequently, points were installed at roughly one-mile (1.5km) intervals leading into an inclined runaway spur. These were manned round the clock and the point blades were only moved from the uphill spur once the pointsman was satisfied that the train was under control. An elaborate whistle code alerted him to a train in

Opposite: The 10,495ft (3,199m) high Mount Stephen towers over a freight train on the western approach to Kicking Horse Pass.

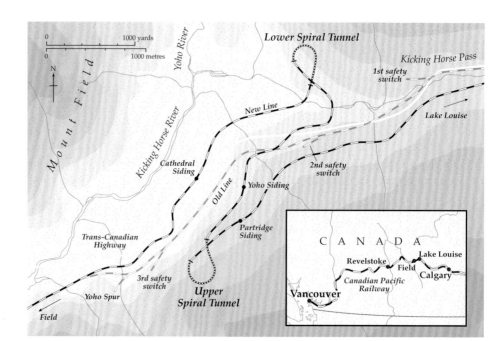

difficulty or reassured him that the driver had a hold on it. Naturally a train out of control would still be wrecked at the end of the spur, but as one worker put it: 'Wrecks could take place without hindering traffic on the main line.'

If train crews descended the hill on tenterhooks, it wasn't much better for them in the other direction. The railway settlement at Field was created specifically to deal with the operating challenges posed by the Big Hill. A large stone roundhouse was built to house the banking engines – one locomotive was needed to every five boxcars, and three helpers were needed for the most heavy passenger trains, some cut in mid-train. The locomotives would have been worked to the limit, requiring constant shovelling from the fireman while the driver feared the engine losing its feet and slipping. To avoid having to lug dining-cars up the hill, the CPR built one of its first two hotels at Field as a 'dining station' for

passengers. Half of the 15 bedrooms at Mount Stephen House were for staff, and the others proved so popular that William Van Horne commissioned the English but Canadian-domiciled architect F.M. Rattenbury to enlarge it to accommodate 100 guests in suites with private baths. The upgraded building, also boasting a photographic darkroom for guests' use, opened its doors in 1902.

On 29 September 1901 a series of pictures was taken of the CPR Royal Train of the Duke and Duchess of York (from 1910, George V and Queen Mary). To gain the best possible view of the spectacular scenery, some dignitaries chose (and were permitted) to ride on the buffer beam of the leading locomotive. One photo shows six members

Below: Five locomotives work the royal train on 4 October 1901, caught leaving Field by Edward Whymper, who was writing about and photographing the Rockies (the 'new Switzerland') for the CPR.

Above: The Spiral Tunnels put an end to trains over the Big Hill. One of the 36 Selkirk 2-10-4s is seen leaving the lower tunnel in what is almost certainly a posed photograph – passenger trains were not as long as freights.

Opposite: Members of the royal party of the Duke and Duchess of York at Glacier in 1901. Lady Macdonald, during her similar ride, could 'think of nothing but the novelty, the excitement, and the fun of this mad ride in glorious sunshine and intoxicating air'.

of the royal party on the buffer beam, wrapped up in travelling rugs. Among the photographers recording the separate trains of the Governor-General and the royal party was Edward Whymper who, 36 years previously, had led the first, fateful ascent of the Matterhorn. To make sure they got up the 'Big Hill' from Field without difficulty, five locomotives were used at various places in the trains to distribute their weight and reduce the strain on couplings.

It was apparently Agnes Macdonald, the second wife of Canada's first Prime Minster Sir John Macdonald, who established a vogue for riding on the front buffer beam. In July 1886 the couple were travelling across the country together for the first time. Sir John was worn out by the struggle to get the line built and was reclusive, but his wife announced at Laggan that she wanted to experience the line from the front, and had a platform built over the buffer beam with a chair fixed to it to give her an unimpeded view of the railway. Despite her husband's reservations, her will prevailed. How far she travelled in this exhilarating manner does not appear to have been recorded, but she must have been a lady with plenty of chutzpah.

The Big Hill was in operation for 23 years, and though there were several catastrophic wrecks, they involved freight trains and not a single passenger was killed. The Spiral Tunnels opened on 1 September 1909, bringing to a close one of the most extraordinary exhibitions of steam locomotive power.

MILWAUKEE ROAD'S PACIFIC EXTENSION

KNOWN AS THE Milwaukee Road, the Chicago, Milwaukee & Saint Paul Railroad gained its name in 1874, made up of various constituents. It gradually extended its reach to the Missouri River and Kansas City, and by 1889 was grand enough to move its headquarters into the first all-steel skyscraper in the US, the Rand McNally Building in Chicago. In 1905 it made a bold and – in railway-building terms – very late decision to build a new line of over 1,800 route miles (2,880km) to link Chicago and Puget Sound on the Pacific coast, in order to maintain the railroad's competitiveness. Construction began the following year, and the builders had to cross the Rocky and Cascade mountain ranges to reach Seattle, requiring major engineering works – and a logistical challenge in feeding 10,000 workers strung out across virgin wilderness.

Funded by bond issues, the last of the country's transcontinental railroads was completed in 1909, and trains began serving Seattle and Tacoma. The principal services over the new railway were the daily Olympian and the slower Colombian, which began on 28 May 1911. They were the first all-steel trains in the Pacific North West, and the Olympian took 72 hours between Chicago and Seattle, reduced to 70 from 1926.

Opposite: The Olympian Hiawatha was launched on 29 June 1947 with a mix of heavy and lightweight cars, hauled by diesel locomotives manufactured by Fairbanks-Morse. It was an odd choice. Though the company had made internal combustion engines since the 1890s, it had made its first diesel locomotive as recently as 1944.

Quite apart from the colossal contemporary cost of $60 million, operation of the line proved difficult and costly thanks to steep gradients, sharp curves and temperatures of -40°F (-40°C) in Montana which impaired the efficiency of steam locomotives. The response was the country's first two long-distance electrification schemes – introduced for economic rather than environmental reasons – at 3,000V DC. Using hydroelectricity, the first came into operation in 1915–16 over 440 miles (704km) between Harlowton, Montana, and Avery, Idaho. It was sufficiently successful for the go-ahead to be given for wiring the 216 miles (346km) between Othello and Tacoma in Washington, bringing the total to 656 miles (1,050km) – the longest electrified route mileage of any railway in the world at that time. It became an attraction in its own right: Thomas A. Edison complimented the smooth ride; the baseball player Babe Ruth posed in the cab; in 1923 President Warren G. Harding took the controls en route from Sappington to Avery; and engineers from at least 17 countries are known to have inspected the pioneering system. Its first electric locomotive design, built by General Electric, even had regenerative braking. The benefits of electrification were promoted in the Milwaukee's advertising, which proclaimed that passengers could stand on the open verandas of the observation cars (introduced c.1915) during the summer months without fear of coal cinders.

The railroad passed through lightly populated farming country – its prairie settlements often created by the coming of the railway, and their stations dominated by grain elevators and sidings into stockyards. Some

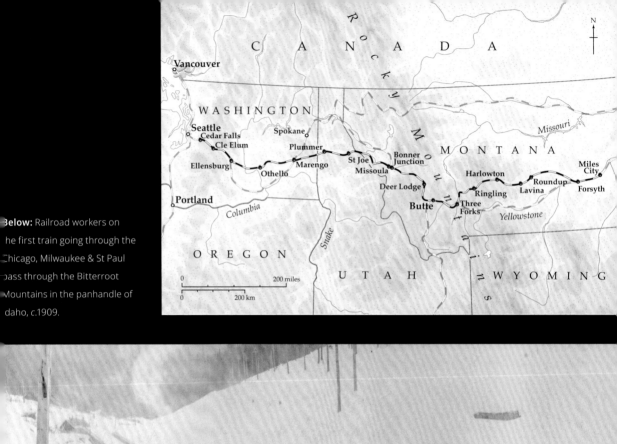

Below: Railroad workers on the first train going through the Chicago, Milwaukee & St Paul pass through the Bitterroot Mountains in the panhandle of Idaho, c.1909.

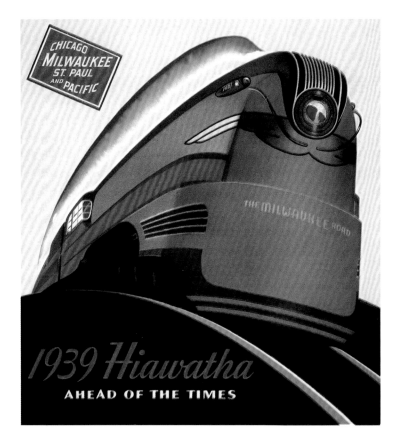

places were named after members of the Rockefeller family, which was a principal shareholder, but not all thrived, and the failures became names known only by railroad workers.

One day not to have been travelling on the Milwaukee was 12 June 1924 – when the largest train robbery in US history took place at Rondout, Illinois, carried out by four brothers known as the 'Newton gang' and four accomplices. Two of the men 'riding the rods' (outside) got onto the footplate as the train approached Rondout and, at gunpoint, forced the crew to stop the train beside waiting cars. The felons threw bottles of formaldehyde through the windows of the passenger cars to incapacitate the 17 armed mail clerks, and made off with $2 million worth of cash and securities. In the melee, one of the Newtons was accidentally shot by a fellow-conspirator, and the gang was arrested while seeking medical help in Chicago – along with a corrupt postal inspector who

Above: A 1939 art deco poster advertising the The Hiawatha, using the striking outline of the railway's semi-streamlined 4-6-4s which had 110½-ton tenders carried on six-wheel bogies at the leading end and four at the back.

Right: The first electric locomotive to arrive on the Milwaukee Road was No. 10200, built by Alco with General Electric components. It was the largest electric locomotive in the world and the first to employ regenerative braking.

had himself sent dozens of thieves to prison for similar crimes.

It was 1928 before the Milwaukee added 'Pacific' to its name – as part of a reorganization following its bankruptcy in 1925. This insolvency, caused by an inability to pay the bonds that had fallen due, did not put a stop to investment; new funding allowed new Pullman-Standard-built cars to appear on the Olympian in 1927. They were finished in an orange and maroon livery, and equipped with roller bearings and radio receivers for broadcasts.

The railroad was proud of the prestige of its top Hiawatha trains and reputation for high-quality service. A Milwaukee employee wrote to his father in January 1939: 'Our Hiawathas are establishing many records in the number of passengers carried, and rank at the top among the nation's trains in earnings per mile. They also attract large crowds who line up along the right-of-way just north of Chicago to see them flash by. It seems our Speedliners have a fascination for young and old alike.'

Above: The interior of a Milwaukee Road dining-car in a classically contrived publicity photograph with nothing as messy as food and drink to be seen.

After the Second World War the Milwaukee upgraded the Olympian, adding Hiawatha to denote the change, though not all the new cars were available for the June 1947 launch: 'Unfortunately the Olympian Hiawatha as it left Chicago and Seattle is not the dreamliner it will be in a few months. The coaches, Touralux sleepers, Tip Top Grill and dining-car, were all beautiful new streamlined cars fresh from the Milwaukee shops. But, alas, the Pullman Car Manufacturing Company could not make delivery of the private-room sleepers and Skytop Lounge. Regardless – the present demand for space indicates it will be a most popular service. And so the Hiawatha fleet goes transcontinental in a big way.'

Some of the cars were built by the Milwaukee's own Menomonee Valley workshops to the design of Brooks

Below: For the inaugural run of the Olympian Hiawatha from Seattle in June 1947, the conductor, engineer and second man were in formal attire for the occasion.

Bottom: One of the Skytop Lounge cars photographed at Glenview, Illinois in 1964. Some were sleeping-observation cars.

Stevens – also known for Harley-Davidson motorbike and Studebaker car designs; each Skytop Lounge car had multiple rows of windows in its tail, and a four-seat wood panelled drawing-room at the other end. As passenger losses mounted with air and road competition, the Olympian Hiawatha was discontinued on 22 May 1961, but some of the Skytop Lounge cars were preserved.

With consummate bad timing, the railroad shut down the power on its electrified sections and became 100 per cent diesel in 1973–4, at the height of the oil crisis when fuel prices soared. To counter rising overheads, maintenance was cut back and the Pacific Extension deteriorated. By 1977 the railroad was bankrupt again, leading to the decision to close 2,000 miles (3,200km) of track between Miles City, Montana, and Cedar Falls, Washington from 29 February 1980: the largest single railroad abandonment in the history of the US. Much of the trackbed has been converted into trails, and some buildings survive as cafés, B&Bs or civic landmarks such as the clock-towered station building at Great Falls, Montana.

COLORADO–DENVER & RIO GRANDE

TALK OF THE narrow gauge in the US and the state that springs to mind is Colorado, though others, such as Maine and Oregon, also had fascinating systems. But the Denver & Rio Grande Railroad (D&RG) was in a league of its own for scale, scenery and colourful history. The last was helped by its founding father, the Anglophile General William Jackson Palmer, who founded Colorado Springs and set up the Denver & Rio Grande Railway in 1870. His intention, never fulfilled, was to build a line south from Denver to El Paso. The following year he visited Wales's Festiniog Railway (originally built to transport slate) while on his honeymoon, and became convinced of the advantages of the narrow gauge for narrow-contoured terrain, though he adopted a 3ft (914mm) gauge rather than the Festiniog's 1ft 11½in (597mm).

The first section, between Denver and Colorado Springs, opened in October 1871, but the decision to turn westward rather continue south to El Paso brought the company into competition for the right to build certain routes. Both physical and legal battles were fought between the D&RG and its arch-rival, the Atchison, Topeka & Santa Fe Railway – the D&RG losing Raton Pass but winning the Royal Gorge beside the Arkansas River. A network of lines was built up, in standard as well as narrow gauge, with the D&RG's main line linking Denver and Salt Lake City. Expansion proved too rapid, and the costs of building the railway through the Black Canyon

Opposite: The Black Canyon at the Gunnison Bridge, Colorado, c.1880 by William Henry Jackson (1843–1942), a prolific railroad photographer, celebrating the achievement of their engineers.

Above: A D&RGW train passes through the spectacular Royal Gorge, Colorado, in 1929. The canyon of the Arkansas River can now be seen from the Royal Gorge Route Railroad sightseeing train.

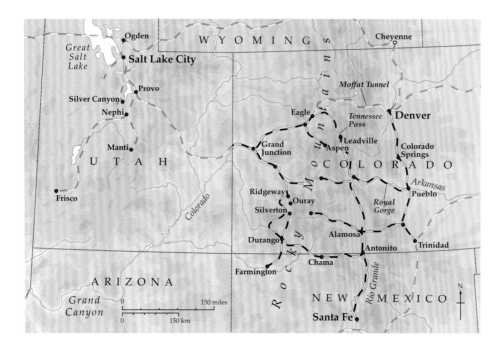

of the Gunnison on the route that eventually linked Mears and Montrose proved its undoing, even if the line deserved its marketing slogan 'Scenic Line of the World'.

The San Juan Extension linking Alamosa with Durango was built as quickly as possible to exploit the mineral boom at Silverton, with numerous curves and loops that were slated for straightening out in a future that never came. The line crossed the Continental Divide at Azotea, and the *lowest* point on the line between Alamosa and Durango was 6,013ft (1,833m) above sea level. Chama, today the headquarters of the Cumbres & Toltec Scenic Railroad, was the principal station between Alamosa and Durango, with a roundhouse which was home to the line's rotary snow-plough. Eastbound trains in particular faced a tough 15½-mile (25km) slog up to the Cumbres Pass, often requiring double-heading or banking, while westbound trains from Antonito had 50 miles of steady climbing. At Cumbres station was a wye (for turning assisting locomotives) with the rare feature of a wooden snow shelter over the reversing tracks. Huge wooden drum water towers resting on a frame replenished the locomotives' tanks.

The D&RG went into receivership in 1884, only a

year after taking a lease on the Denver & Rio Grande Western Railway which General Palmer had set up in Salt Lake City to push eastwards from Provo in Utah. The D&RGW also went into receivership but emerged in 1886, as did the reincorporated Denver & Rio Grande Railroad with British and American shareholders. Construction of narrow-gauge lines through south-western Colorado continued, including the picturesque Rio Grande Southern (RGS) which closed the circuit by linking Durango and Ridgeway. Eventually there were 675 miles (1,080km) of narrow-gauge track.

The southerly San Juan Extension was at its busiest from 1882 to 1893, when the silver mines at Silverton – over 40 of them at one time – were generating huge volumes of ore outbound and supplies inbound. Mining of gold and other ores compensated for the losses following the Silver Panic of 1893, but declining volumes and revenue had already begun.

In one of those costly strategic decisions arising out of the unplanned development of a railway network, the 48-mile (77km) Farmington branch south from Durango was built to standard gauge to try to thwart the ambitions of a rival. When the threat had passed, it was narrowed in

1923. The line threaded semi-arid hill country populated with cottonwoods, and served ranching areas.

Even though a four-day Narrow Gauge Circuit was created for tourists after the First World War, taking in the scenic delights of Marshall Pass, the Black Canyon, Lizard Head, the Curecanti Needle and the seven trestles and spiral of Ophir, costs continued to exceed revenue on several lines, and shut-down – at least to passengers – was considered before the 1920s were out. More creative management delayed execution, but the redirecting of traffic over standard-gauge lines and road competition led to the closure of Gunnison to Montrose to passengers in the mid-1930s, and the last freight ran in 1949. Much of the trackbed now lies under a reservoir.

A landslide in 1947 finally broke the narrow-gauge circuit, and the Sapinero-Cedar Creek section of the old Marshall Pass line was abandoned. Mine closures (or a switch to trucks), and cancellation of the mail contract because of unreliability caused by deferred maintenance put paid to the RGS in 1952. The lines further south survived longer, thanks to traffic in crude oil, livestock, and materials for a newly discovered natural gas and oil field. The D&RG's insufficient stock for carrying the pipes from Pueblo was remedied by adapting standard-gauge flat cars to narrow-gauge configurations, rather than buying new. Survival of the San Juan Extension and the Silverton and Farmington branches allowed two of the most scenic sections to become heritage railways: the Durango & Silverton; and the Cumbres & Toltec between Antonito and Chama, across the border with New Mexico.

Below: The west side of Marshall Pass in 1881 by William Henry Jackson. Beside his commissioned work for the Union Pacific and the Baltimore & Ohio railroads, Jackson travelled the world for the short-lived World's Transportation Commission.

For those who rode the rails, the narrow gauge never offered the comfort of the standard gauge, even during the halcyon inter-war years when quality was the watchword to winning business. But the open-platform coaches would have offered a wider view of the landscapes, and those receptive to such things must have found charm in the kerosene lamps – and even in the coal stove that provided heat. Some improvements were effected after yet another bankruptcy in 1935, and three parlor cars even had stainless-steel galleys and dinette sections fitted.

The end came for all but the two heritage sections in 1967, when closure of the San Juan Extension between Alamosa and Durango and the Farmington branch was authorized, bringing an end to the use of steam by the country's Class 1 railroads on 6 December the following year. The Cumbres & Toltec Scenic Railroad and the Durango & Silverton Narrow Gauge Railroad are engagingly redolent of the great days of the US's largest narrow-gauge network. Thanks to them, it requires little imagination to conjure up the days when one could board the *San Juan* express between Alamosa and Durango, have lunch with wine served in the parlor car *Chama*, and take coffee in an armchair in the foothills of the San Juan Mountains.

Opposite: Clear Creek Canyon, c.1899 by William Henry Jackson, was on another 3ft gauge line linked to the D&RG, the Colorado Central to Golden and Georgetown.

Above: A typical post-war scene on the D&RG in its final years. Taken on 2 July, a K36 2-8-2 stands by one of the bulbous water towers that were found throughout the railroad.

VIRGINIA & TRUCKEE RAILROAD

LUCIUS BEEBE, WHO knew a thing or two about US railroads, described the Virginia & Truckee (V&T) as 'the most glamorous and romantic railroad in the United States', though, like many other lines, its origins were cloaked in financial machinations of dubious probity. It ran from a junction with the Central Pacific at Reno to Carson City, where the final third of the railway began its snaking course into the hills to Virginia City. In 1905, when its prosperity was already waning, it built a 15-mile (24km) branch south to Minden to tap into the area's dairy farming.

The V&T had its origins in gold and silver. In 1859 a lump of 'blue stuff' was sent from what became Virginia City to California for analysis; the blue mud turned out to be practically pure silver with some gold, and was assayed at $4,500. News of the Comstock Lode, described as 'the most prodigious bonanza in the history of the world', spread like wildfire, and over 25,000 Californians had crossed the Sierra Mountains by the following summer. Mark Twain soon joined them, cutting his teeth as a journalist on Virginia City's newspaper after failing as a miner. It was not all plain sailing; the first bonanza was almost worked out by 1865, but the downturn gave four men, who knew there was far more to come, the chance to gain control over the reducing mills.

Opposite: Baldwin 4-6-0 No. 27 of 1913, the last locomotive purchased by the V&T, shunts freight cars. The locomotive is now displayed at the Nevada State Railroad Museum in Carson City, having been withdrawn from service on 1 October 1948.

William Sharon, as the local agent of the Bank of California, did this by extending credit to distressed mill owners before foreclosing on them and wrapping seven of the mills into the Union Mining & Milling Co., to be followed by 10 more. Soon it was a case of 'use the bank's mills or no credit'.

Sharon soon had the city and the mills sewn up – and then, in 1869, he commissioned a railroad to Reno from an engineer who had never even thought of building one. Locomotives were ordered from San Francisco and Philadelphia and dragged by teams of oxen to Carson City and Virginia City. For all his financial acumen, Sharon liked a party – and the liberality of his liquid hospitality was enjoyed at various stages in the railroad's progress.

Within three years trains were travelling over rails rolled in Sheffield, Yorkshire, and helping to reopen closed mines by lowering transport costs. In the early 1870s, the further discoveries correctly anticipated by Sharon and his partners were realized in such spectacular fashion that the period became known as the Big Bonanza. Trains of ore made their way to the stamping mills on the Carson River which became as dense as the steel mills of Pittsburgh.

Besides carrying huge quantities of freight, the V&T's yellow and green carriages were also earning good money from leisure. They took parties to picnics at the mansion of a prospector whose widow had turned its grounds into a place of recreation with gardens and swimming pool. The granite twelve-road roundhouse in Carson City became the venue for the Fourth of July Independence Day ball, and was adorned with bunting,

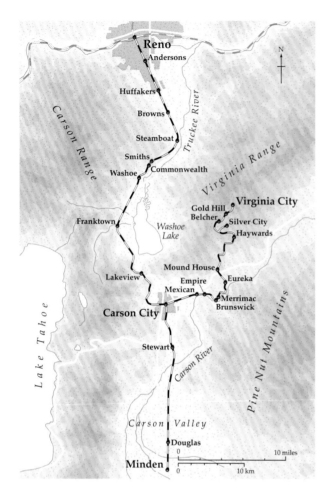

artificial flowers, Japanese lanterns and decorative plaques. A baggage car almost full of Louis Roederer champagne was hauled in to make sure the festivities went with a swing. People from all the railroad's communities came to dance to a band hired for the then huge sum of $250, and feast on oysters, lobster, quail and venison. A journalist on a local paper waxed lyrical about the whole affair, reporting that every inch in the floor laid over the rails in the engine shed had been 'nicely planed [so] that the fantastic toe may encounter no slightest obstacle, and the entire idea approaches the confines of the sublime.'

Sharon had become known as 'King of the Comstock' and was wealthy through the railroad as well as from silver. By 1873 there were over 30 trains a day between Carson and Virginia cities, helping to generate a profit of $100,000 a month for the V&T's three shareholders, and making their company the richest railway in the world in terms of return on capital. The Central Pacific was reluctant to allow its Silver Palace sleeping-cars over the hilly curves and grades of the V&T until George Pullman himself arrived at Virginia City in his own private car. Soon after, a sleeping-car service began between Oakland and Virginia City for bankers and businessmen. By the mid-1870s there were 52 trains a day, and railroad staff were taking in so much money they had to be

Left: A measure of the traffic once handled by the V&T is given by the size of its engine shed at Carson City, with 12 roads. Located between Plaza, Ann, Stewart and Sophia streets, the building was demolished in 1991.

protected by guards with sawn-off shotguns. The trains also had armed guards, though none were apparently in attendance at one of the last great shipments, recorded by photographers, when $1,500,000 in gold bars were moved out of the assay office in 1917. In one of those curious calculations loved by the media, it is estimated that the V&T hauled its own weight – of stock, rail and bridge – in silver, and that in monetary terms it hauled $600 million in silver and gold. Much of it went into creating the public realm of San Francisco as well as its mansions.

Yet even by 1879 there were signs that the peak has been passed, though profitable mining continued for at least two more decades. Declining revenues were cushioned by the pockets of its owner, the grandson of one of its founders, who kept a railway establishment that exceeded the strict needs of the traffic. After his death in 1927, the liquidator tightened belts but kept

the railroad going. An end to the line between Carson and Virginia cities came through geology rather than economics, though a reluctance to fix the settling tunnels was naturally influenced by inadequate returns. The last whistle in Virginia City sounded in 1938, and the railway entered its twilight years – operating a two-coach passenger service and hauling merchandise and the output of Minden's dairies.

Even when the train service was down to one a day in the 1940s, Beebe thought the V&T train 'possessed of a flourish, a display of pioneer elegance which even the *City of San Francisco* [the streamlined Chicago–Oakland train] flashing through Reno on an adjacent track in a torrent of de luxe upholstery cannot hope to imitate.' But time on the railway was called in 1950 when most of the track was lifted and the equipment sold.

Interest in reviving the line began in the 1970s, culminating, on 14 August 2009, in the first train running from Gold Hill to Carson City in 68 years. The line uses two Baldwin-built locomotives, a 2-8-2 of 1914 and a 2-8-0 of 1916. In Carson City is the Nevada State Railroad Museum: its collection includes 65 locomotives and cars, 40 of them built before 1900, and rides are offered on selected days. Besides three V&T steam locomotives, it has the V&T's extraordinary petrol-powered railcar built in 1910 by the McKeen Motor Car Company in Omaha. Registered as a National Historic Landmark, this has a distinctive maroon body with circular windows and a V-shaped 'wind-splitter' front end. The idea of this vehicle achieving a speed that would benefit from an aerodynamic shape is wholly in keeping with the V&T's grandiose past.

Right: No. 29 on the restored Virginia & Truckee Railroad south of Virginia City in March 2010. Built by Baldwin in 1916, the 2-8-0 came from the Longview, Portland & Northern Railway in Oregon and Washington.

Below: The derelict remains of the V&T's oldest locomotive, 2-6-0 No. 1 *Lyon*, built in 1869 by H.J. Booth & Co. in San Francisco, which was also known as Union Iron Works. No. 1 had two identical sisters.

FLORIDA EAST COAST RAILWAY

NO RAILWAY IN THE world has given its passengers the sensation of being at sea like the one linking Miami and Key West. This extraordinary line strode across the waters of the Gulf of Mexico for over 100 miles, much of it on viaduct. It was the creation of one of the lesser-known 'robber barons' from the buccaneering days of 19th-century American capitalism.

Henry Morrison Flagler (1830–1913) had been a founder of Standard Oil, in partnership with John D. Rockefeller and Henry Huttleston Rogers, building up the world's largest oil refinery until the company was declared an illegal monopoly by the Supreme Court in 1911. Long before Standard Oil was broken up, Flagler had developed interests in Florida during visits for the sake of his wife's health. He bought up short-line railroads that would later become part of the Florida East Coast Railway (FECR), with a southern terminus at West Palm Beach.

Two hard winters in 1894 and 1895 made Flagler consider a move south, since the area now occupied by Miami had escaped the freeze and damage to the region's orange groves. Land grants were offered as an inducement for an extension of the railway, and the head of steel reached Biscayne Bay in 1896, being named Mayaimi from an old Indian word. Flagler became known as the Father of Miami, developing orange growing as well as tourism.

Construction of the Panama Canal and the enhanced prospects for the port of Key West, 128 miles (205km) beyond the end of the Florida peninsula, encouraged Flagler to commission surveys into an extension of the railway. One survey party examined the Everglades area, south of Homestead, which then covered 8,000 square miles (20,720 sq km) and was home to panthers as well as alligators and crocodiles; while the other determined whether a line could be built along the string of small islands, or 'keys'.

Opposite: The journey across the viaducts and embankments looks delightful on a balmy day, but it must have been a different sensation when a storm was raging and waves showered the carriages.

Right: Seven Mile Bridge stretches to the horizon. Teams taking out inspection trolleys must have been exceptionally careful to make sure there were no unscheduled extra workings.

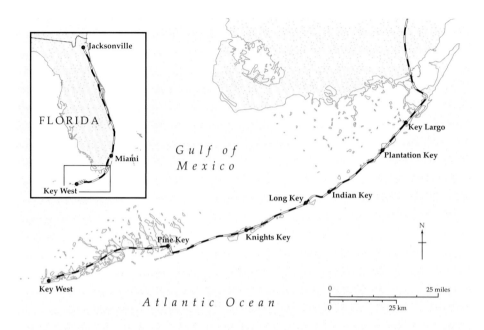

Having been told it could, Flagler had contractors at work by April 1905, with Joseph Meredith as Engineer. Huge dredgers created an embankment for the trackbed across the swamps to the sea, where the first of 17 miles (27km) of bridges and 20 miles (32km) of embankment carried the line over the water. The longest of these was Knight's Key Viaduct, which stretched for 7 miles (11.2km), had 335 steel girder spans between concrete piers and 210 concrete arches, and needed to be capable of withstanding hurricanes. Some of the bridges had to be moveable to maintain navigation. Many of the workforce who built these structures lived in dormitories mounted on barges; the boats were also adapted to form floating yards for mixing concrete or assembling steelwork. A hurricane in 1906 broke their mooring cables, sending some out to sea and others to be dashed against the keys and reefs; 70 men were lost. The salt water and air compelled the engineers to apply anti-rust protection even to the rails as well as the steelwork.

After the railway's opening in January 1912, with Henry Flagler in his private coach on the first train, a sleeping-car service was set up between New York, Miami and Key West. Named the *Havana Special*, it provided connections with P&O steamers to Cuba. These vessels also carried loaded freight cars from the FECR. The service prompted construction of resorts along the previously empty keys, but many still saw the line as 'Flagler's Folly' which would never pay its way. The terminus at Key West covered 134 acres (54ha), serving a concrete pier 1,700ft (518m) long.

One of the early travellers on the *Havana Special* recalled there being 'nothing more wonderful than swaying from side to side surrounded by all that beautiful water. The dining-car had linens, big napkins, wonderful food. And besides being such an experience, the train was faster than driving.' Fishermen came to the camp built for them at Long Key, but the scarcity of fresh water inhibited development on the scale that would pay dividends. Besides passengers, freight cars went south with manufactured goods and race horses for Cuba, and returned with pineapples (sometimes 100 cars of them in season) as well as tanks of sugar and molasses. Perhaps the most extraordinary train was the daily service from Everglade station carrying dozens of conical wooden containers – each holding 3,000 gallons (13,638 litres) of water – to replenish tanks between Jewfish and Key West.

On Labor Day 1935 a Category 5 hurricane devastated the keys and swept away 40 miles of track. The insolvent FECR could not fund reconstruction, so the route was sold to the State of Florida, which used the trackbed as the basis of the Overseas Highway, part of US 1 linking Fort Kent in Maine and Key West. Some of the old bridges form part of the 106-mile (171km) Florida Keys Overseas Heritage Trail.

Above: A truss-girder section of the line with missing span, perhaps removed for navigation though the 1935 storm destroyed some parts as well as track.

Left: Florida East Coast Railway No. 10 with station and train staff at San Mateo. Flagler hoped that the railway would carry coal to the bunkering station at Key West for ships steaming to South America. By the time the line opened, the range of ships had increased, ending such hopes.

Opposite: An advert of c.1913 extolling the virtues of Florida's resorts and their facilities as well as the new Pullman service to reach the Panama Canal.

FLORIDA EAST COAST

Every Day a June Day, Full of Sunshine
Where Winter Exists In Memory Only

The famous Winter Resorts of the East Coast of Florida furnish a greater variety of attractions than any other resort section of the world. Unequalled opportunities for outdoor life and its many diversions. **Golf** on the finest links in the country; **Tennis** on clay courts always in condition; **Surf Bathing** in water at a temperature of 70 degrees and upward; **Horseback Riding** and **Motoring** over well built roads, amid picturesque tropical scenery, or on the hard sandy beach; **Yachting, Rowing** and **Fishing** in the deep sea and land-locked waters; all kinds of **Game**—from quail to deer—for the most enthusiastic hunter; **Chair Wheeling** and bicycling on palm lined promenades, and through tropical jungles.

FINEST AND HEALTHIEST CLIMATE IN THE WORLD
—— THE PRINCIPAL RESORTS AND HOTELS ——

PONCE DE LEON	. . . St. Augustine	ROYAL POINCIANA	. . . Palm Beach
ALCAZAR	. . . St. Augustine	THE BREAKERS	. . . . . Palm Beach
ORMOND	. . . Ormond-on-the-Halifax	ROYAL PALM	. . . . Miami

LONG KEY FISHING CAMP—AMONG THE FLORIDA KEYS
THE COLONIAL, Nassau, Bahama Islands
Desirable accommodations at all points to meet any disposition or demand.

New Route to the Panama Canal

The Oversea Railroad to Key West, one of the marvels of the 20th Century, has opened up a new and shorter route to Uncle Sam's latest and greatest enterprise, the Panama Canal, connecting at Key West via palatial steamers, sailing twice monthly for Colon, Panama.

Through Pullman Service from principal cities to Jacksonville and Key West, with connections to all Resorts on the **FLORIDA EAST COAST.** For Complete Detailed Information, Booklets, Tickets, Reservations, apply to Local Agent or

243 Fifth Avenue
NEW YORK   **FLORIDA EAST COAST**   109 West Adams St.
CHICAGO
General Offices, ST. AUGUSTINE, FLORIDA

AFRICA

MASSAWA–AGORDAT

THE FUTILITY OF endless road building has persuaded many governments to reopen railway lines, but few countries have done so on such a grand scale as Ecuador and Eritrea. The Andean railway from Guayaquil to Quito now carries tourists and local passengers again, but the Eritrean story has been less happy.

Colonized by Italy in the 1880s, Eritrea has some of the most inhospitable and barren places on earth. Just across its border with Ethiopia lies the Danakil Depression; it is 100m (328ft) below sea level and the hottest place on earth, yet Eritrea's capital of Asmara is the highest in Africa at 2,325m (7,628ft). A railway that climbs from sea level to a summit of 2,394m (7,854ft) within 117km (73 miles) was thought to be impossible without the use of a rack, but Italian engineers eventually found an adhesion-only route through the mountains to create one of Africa's most scenic railways.

The 950mm (3ft 1⅜in) gauge line runs for 306.4km (191.7 miles) from Massawa on the Red Sea to Agordat, and is the only one of the country's three railways to have survived into the 21st century. It was built between 1887 and 1932 with a gauge chosen to allow second-hand locomotives and rolling stock to be drawn from narrow-gauge lines in Italy, Sicily or Sardinia. The ruling gradient over the 117km (73 miles) from the coast to Asmara was 1 in 28, and even the 0-4-4-0 Mallets which hauled most trains were limited to a payload of 90 tons between Ghinda and Asmara. The restricted capacity of the railway encouraged construction of the longest

cableway ever built, stretching for 71.8km (45 miles) between Massawa and Asmara. Opened in 1937, some of its equipment was removed as war reparations by the British.

The journey by steam train took 10 hours, so those unimpressed by the sight and sound of the engines' demonstrative exertions must have been delighted when a 'littorina' service by Fiat diesel railcar reduced its time to 4 hours in the mid-1930s. A doyen of American train travel writers, Charles Small, was fully open to the experience when he travelled in the 1950s, despite encountering carriages which 'have hard wooden seats and are crammed with the locals, who betray little familiarity with soap and water. It is a magnificent trip up the hill complete with smoke, cinders, exhaust beats and the high-pitched squeak of the continental type steam whistle, all in the best tradition.' He regarded the littorina as rather 'effete', but did appreciate the bar dispensing warm beer, an amenity 'not to be regarded lightly in the Red Sea heat'. Not being of a nervous disposition, he even relished the sight of three policemen, each carrying a Lee-Enfield .303 rifle with a cartridge in its breech, who travelled on the train to defend it against *shiftas* (bandits).

Between Massawa and Asmara there are 30 tunnels (one a rock shelter), 35 major viaducts and bridges, and 13 stations. Leaving Massawa across a causeway, the railway crosses a coastal plain of acacia bushes, a few palms and scrubby sycamores. Small described the wind whipping 'across one's face like an oxy-acetylene flame. Even the warm beer served aboard furnishes only temporary relief for parched throats and lips'. Between Mai Atal and Damas there is a hump which required trains to be split. By Ghinda and its orchards of tangerines, the

Opposite: Reflecting the line's history, many of the locomotives on the Eritrea Railway were built in Italy. An 0-4-4-0T of Class R440, built by the Ansaldo company in Genoa in 1915, nears Arbaroba in 2014.

Right: One of the Fiat littorina railcars passes one of the railway's more bizarre rock formations. The railcars more than halved the journey time.

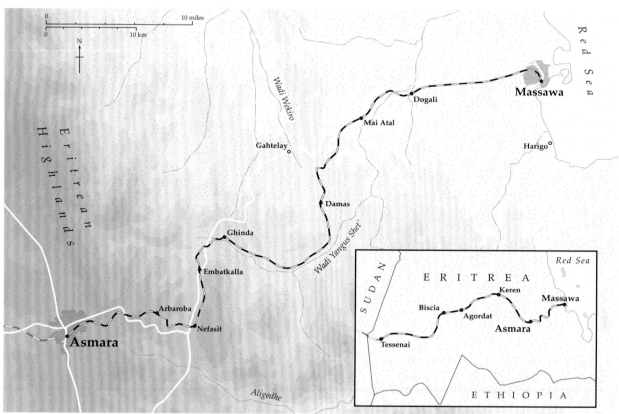

sting has gone out of the sun and the vegetation is much more luxuriant. The most dramatic section is between Nefasit, Arbaroba and the summit, with three horseshoe loops and 20 tunnels, the line clinging to a ledge above sheer drops with a blue haze of mountains receding to the horizon. There is a slight descent from the summit to Asmara and the railway's main workshops.

Beyond the Italian, model capital city, there are nine tunnels, 30 bridges and 17 stations. As the line crosses the upland plateau west of Dem Sebai, herds of goats and donkeys can be seen among giant wild fig trees. The line drops to Keren, 220km (137½ miles) from Massawa and 1,390m (4,560ft) above sea level, where the country's main battle of the Second World War was fought. Once through the Keren Gorge, the line descends through the desert region of sand and camels stretching to the border and journey's end at Agordat, at 606m (1,988ft) above sea level. Though the railway was built beyond Agordat to

Biscia, close to the border with Sudan, it was used only for military supplies and was lifted in 1942 by British troops. It was the original intention to extend the railway to an interchange with the 1067mm (3ft 6in) gauge railway from Kassala in Sudan which crossed the border with Eritrea to reach Tessenei, but the Italian focus during the 1930s was on the conquest of Ethiopia.

The line was at its busiest in the mid-1930s when there were 38 trains a day between Massawa and Asmara in both directions, and the railway was the largest employer in the country. Following the Battle of Keren in February–April 1941, the Italians surrendered, and the railway remained under British administration until

Below: The railway from Massawa on the Red Sea to Asmara traverses some stirring scenery on the way, exemplified by this view of a Class R442 0-4-4-0T at the Devil's Gate on its way up to Asmara.

Eritrea's federated status with Ethiopia was established in 1952. A paper by the British Assistant Chief Mechanical Engineer of Sudan Government Railways looked at ways of augmenting the locomotive fleet in Eritrea following the Italian capitulation; he identified redundant locomotives on the Irish 3ft (914mm) gauge railways which could be converted to run in Eritrea, but it proved possible to rehabilitate the railway using the Italian engines without recourse to imports.

The most powerful locomotives in the fleet of 64 were the 0-4-4-0 Mallet tanks. The first three were compounds supplied in 1907 by Maffei of Munich, and three were built by Asmara works in the 1930s, but the rest were built by Ansaldo at Genoa – 13 in 1911–15 and another eight in compound form in 1938. There were also five Klien-Lindner 0-8-0Ts, designed to negotiate tight radius curves, but the British found them so prone to derailing that they stopped using them. There were also various 2-6-0, 0-6-0 and 0-4-0 tanks, plus the 11 Fiat art deco railcars.

The wildlife and railway artist Terence Cuneo visited the country in 1973 to paint two pictures of the railway, and arrived at his hotel so covered in coal dust that 'the hall porter did all in his power to remove me from the premises'. He just caught the finale before the railway closed in January 1976 and its infrastructure was allowed to deteriorate or was gradually removed.

Following independence in 1991, after three decades of violent struggle between liberation parties and against Ethiopia, the government decided in 1994 to rebuild the railway, which had suffered badly from the ravages of war. The work was undertaken by men on National Service, directed by retired railwaymen, and three Mallets and two Breda 0-4-0Ts were refurbished

Opposite: A short goods train, run by FarRail for the benefit of a visiting group of photographers, winds its way up towards the summit of the line. In its heyday the Eritrea railway was primarily a goods line.

Below: Mallet tanks were well suited to the sharp curves of the railway. The front of such locomotives were supported on an articulated Bissell truck, devised by the Swiss engineer Anatole Mallet.

in the main workshops at Asmara. The project ended in 2003, but only Massawa to Asmara was rebuilt, and the anticipated freight traffic has never materialized.

Sunday excursions were scheduled down the mountain from Asmara to Arbaroba, and many charter trains were operated over the whole length of the line for overseas groups intent on photographing this phoenix. One organizer, Bernd Seiler of FarRail Tours, went so far as obtaining a shipment of coal when lack of fuel was presented as an obstacle to a charter in 2014. Each visit may be the last due to floods and landslides, the lamentable condition of the locomotives, and the death of those long-retired railwaymen with the skills to do something about it. Some knowledge was passed on to a younger generation, but it is extremely unlikely that scheduled journeys will ever be revived or trains run again west of Asmara.

Above: Builders plate from one of the last remaining Ansaldo built 0-4-4-0 Mallet tank locomotives, works No. 1366 built in 1938. The Ansaldo name appeared on engineering products from 1852 to 2015.

PORT ELIZABETH– AVONTUUR

UNTIL THE DEREGULATION of freight transport between 1977 and 1990, South African Railways carried the lion's share of the country's freight, to the great benefit of the environment and reduction of road death statistics. Reliance on the railways was reflected in substantial traffic levels even on the country's 2ft (610mm) gauge railways. The longest was in the Eastern Cape and stretched for 177 miles (283km) west from Port Elizabeth to Avontuur, with a branch from Gamtoos to Patensie. It carried colossal amounts of freight – principally fruit until 1985 and limestone until 2001 – which made it a magnet for photographers, along with its impressive landscapes and a viaduct that would not have been out of place on a Cape Gauge main line.

The primary purpose of the railway was to help the fruit farmers of the Gamtoos Valley and the area known as the Langkloof who had previously had to send their produce by wagon over dirt roads. One train would carry the loads of 25 ox-wagons. The farmers' support for the railway translated into gifts of land for it, though these were driven by self-interest, as they knew that its construction would increase their profits and the value of their farms. Approval for the first 2ft gauge line in the colony was given in 1899, and though work began immediately, little was achieved until 1901. The line opened in stages between 1903 and 1907, three years

before the four colonies formed the Union of South Africa and most railways became part of South African Railways (SAR). The 19-mile (30km) branch line up the Gamtoos River valley to Patensie opened in 1914 and tapped another fruit-growing area. Fruit heading for Port Elizabeth included apples, water melons, guavas and pears.

The first engineering challenge was the crossing of the Van Stadens Gorge, and the surveyors had to hack through dense creepers linking the trees before they could take readings. The surveyors were allowed a maximum gradient of 1 in 40, which challenged their skill in devising a feasible descent from Summit to Loerie. In a parallel with construction of the railway to Alice Springs (see p.97), some of the earthworks in and near Port Elizabeth were carried out by men wholly unsuited to the task. They were British subjects – refugee clerks, bakers and shop staff – who had fled the fighting further north during the Boer War, and were put to work rather than be a burden to the local populace.

The most extraordinary structure on the line is Van Stadens Bridge, the highest railway bridge in the world carrying a 2ft gauge line. In common with the Victoria Falls Bridge, construction relied on a Blondin cableway once the first and fourth piers had been built. The deck of the 642ft long (196m) viaduct is 256ft (77m) above the river, and the bridge works became a destination for single-coach day excursions hauled by a Manning Wardle 0-4-0T named *Midget*. There was also a 17-span timber bridge across the Gamtoos River.

Though the farmers had eagerly awaited the arrival of the railway, it became evident that the transition from

Opposite: A Kalahari 2-8-2 NG15.17, the first member of the class and fully restored by Sandstone Heritage Trust, crosses the Van Stadens viaduct with the September 2005 4-day Avontuur Adventurer.

N

0   50 miles

0   50 km

Left: Rural passengers continued to use carriages thoughtfully provided on the daily pick-up goods by the operating staff for another 40 years after the advertised service was discontinued *c.* 1947.

Above: The 9-mile climb from Loerie out of the Gamtoos river valley required an engine cut into the middle to help the train engine. The Avontuur railway delivered 1,200 tons of limestone every day to the cement factory near Port Elizabeth.

growing subsistence-scale crops to market gardening would be slow without help. Most unusually, the Cape Government Railways' Superintendent in charge of the line appointed an Agricultural Assistant and an Intelligence Officer whose object was to increase production and therefore railway revenues. The former advised on the best crops for the soil type and imparted new farming methods, while the latter found markets for the produce.

Another unusual aspect of the railway was a consequence of its length and the remoteness of many of the gangers' cottages. A Medical Officer based at Humansdorp was responsible for the health of all employees except those at Humewood Road, the main station in Port Elizabeth. Travelling in his own coach, he covered Humewood Road–Humansdorpon Fridays and Humansdorp to Avontuur on Mondays, his train's locomotive bearing a headboard of a white disc with red cross to signify it was carrying the officer's coach.

Early locomotives included 2-6-4 tanks by Manning Wardle of Leeds and six 4-6-0s from Bagnall of Stoke-on-Trent, but perhaps the most remarkable locomotives to work on the line came during the First World War. After 15 narrow-gauge engines were packed off to occupied German South West Africa, SAR narrow-gauge lines were so short of motive power that nine derelict Lawley 4-4-0s of 1895–8 were rescued from Bamboo Creek on the Beira Railway and overhauled in 1915. Originally 42 of these elegant but diminutive locomotives had been built for the Beira by the Falcon Works at Loughborough in Leicestershire or at Dugald Drummond's short-lived

Glasgow Railway Engineering Co. Three of the nine overhauled locomotives came to work on the Avontuur. (Two survive in working order on the Sandstone Estates railway in the Free State province.)

Before the First World War, six 4-6-0s came from Bagnall in Stafford and three more from Kerr Stuart in Stoke-on-Trent. The war prevented repeat orders so they went to Baldwin in Philadelphia for another six 4-6-0s and even six Pacifics, and in 1920 the first Garratt arrived on trial, though the decision to order these articulated locomotives had been taken before the war. The 2-6-0+0-6-2 was a complete success, hauling the load of two straight engines and therefore halving labour costs, though it was 1928 before the best-known

2-6-2+2-6-2 NGG13s arrived at Humewood Road. SAR never ordered another rigid-framed locomotive for the South African narrow gauge, though the NG15 2-8-2s from South West Africa later appeared on the Avontuur and were known as 'Kalaharis'. Firemen were less than enthusiastic about the Garratt's confined cabs compared with the open cabs of the straight engines; not only were Garratt cabs much hotter, but working closer to the fire-doors singed overalls within weeks, not months. Crews were able to swing a seat outside the cab, giving the

Below: A Class NG 15 on empty wagons pulls away from the siding at Heights in the Langkloof with Mt Formosa in the background.

curious spectacle of seeing a locomotive head-on with driver and firemen sitting outside – their legs dangling over the pathway beside the ballast, so great was the overhang of the locomotives. The main locomotive depot was at Humewood Road where the workshops were sufficiently well equipped to reprofile wheels. There were smaller sheds at Humansdorp and Patensie, and a sub-shed was added at Loerie. The shed at Assegaaibos was dramatically upgraded in the mid-1960s with an impressive coal stage and crew quarters.

The locomotives had an exacting life. Besides the eastbound steep climb to Van Stadens and the even fiercer westbound climb from Loerie to Summit, from Loerie westward the line climbed almost continuously to Avontuur at 2,859ft (871m) above sea level. Its path was exacerbated by numerous minimum-radius horseshoe curves, and most freights were loaded to their maximum permitted tonnage. The scenery for much of the way was of tree-lined watercourses along valley floors flanked by green hillsides rising to rocky summits.

In the early years a launch was put on the Gamtoos River to tow a lighter of agricultural produce from the opposite bank from the railway, and this vessel extended its worth by carrying weekend excursionists along the river. The railway even hired tents for those wanting a week camping somewhere along the river towards its mouth, which was the destination of one of the offered excursions. Afternoon tea at Thornhill station, as well as dinner, bed and breakfast in a 'first-class hotel' at Humansdorp, was laid on as part of a weekend package. The railway was also expected to attract tourist traffic to the embryonic resort of Jeffreys Bay, and it was just possible to photograph a train with the sea in the background near Kabeljousrivier.

The river was a source of trouble as well as revenue. In 1905 the Eastern Cape was subject to flooding so severe that nothing could move east of Loerie, and the water was 10ft (3m) above rail level at the Gamtoos bridge instead of 15ft (4.5m) below. When the waters receded, nine spans were missing.

A huge boost was given to the railway in 1927 when the Eastern Province Cement Company opened a

works at New Brighton north of Port Elizabeth which was reached by a private 12-mile (19km) line from a junction on the Avontuur line at Chelsea. This created a substantial flow of limestone, first from a quarry at Patensie and then from one near Loerie.

Agriculture and particularly the deciduous fruit industry in the Langkloof prospered to the extent that the train carrying apples to the cooling sheds in Port Elizabeth before export was known as the Apple Express. An all-time record was achieved in 1984 when 58,000 tons of fruit were moved to Port Elizabeth and a letter was sent by the Langkloof producers thanking the railway for its 'truly outstanding service'. Yet the following year, South African Transport Services, the state-owned transport organization, decided the fruit traffic would go by road. Simultaneously the decision was taken that branch lines, and especially those of narrow gauge, should be phased out. The decision was approved by the Minister of Transport, who owned a fleet of trucks. Pressure was applied to the cement company to move the limestone by road instead of rail, but there was uproar about the idea of shifting the Avontuur's 599,700 tons of freight traffic in 1984 onto the road, 384,000 of those tons being limestone. The stone traffic was largely diesel-hauled before it ended in 2001 when the quarry closed.

The potential for reviving the idea of weekend excursion trains was realized in 1965 when the Port Elizabeth Historical Society persuaded SAR to run a special Kalahari-hauled passenger train to Loerie. It was a great success and became a regular weekend departure – bearing the name the Apple Express, and providing a stop for passengers to walk across Van Stadens Bridge. Appropriately the coaches were painted green, the dominant apple species being Golden Delicious. The train became part of the tourist attractions of the Eastern Cape, running even more successfully under the auspices of the private Alfred County Railway from 1993. Regulatory difficulties and the withdrawal of local funding ended 45 years of contributions to the line, with the last run of the Apple Express in December 2010. Efforts are currently being made to revive the train with a pair of NG15 2-8-2 locomotives.

BULAWAYO–LIVINGSTONE

CECIL RHODES' UNREALIZED vision of a railway linking Cape Town and Cairo was the driving force behind many sections of track between South Africa and Egypt. One of these was the line that linked Southern Rhodesia's industrial and railway hub at Bulawayo with what became in 1911 the capital of Northern Rhodesia, Livingstone. In common with most of the railways in southern Africa, the lines of Rhodesia Railways (RR) were built to 3ft 6in (1067mm) gauge, known as Cape Gauge after the colony which adopted it in 1873.

It was the discovery of coal deposits at Wankie that determined the railway's route to the north-west of Bulawayo, and the famous Rhodesian contractor George Pauling set to work in 1901. As far at Dett it was such easy going, through sand veldt, that the 70 miles (112km) between Gwaai and Dett are dead straight, but beyond there it was very different. The forest and bush was so dense that surveyors had to crawl on hands and knees to get through it, and hacking it back to allow their instruments to make the next traverse was tough work, compounded by the risk from game and malarial mosquitoes. The men building the line slept on platforms among tree branches wherever possible, and tents were hedged in with high poles covered with thorn bushes. Once the line opened to Wankie in 1903, it soon became possible to stop importing coal.

Meanwhile George Pauling and the engineer Sir Charles Metcalfe had been prospecting the best place to cross the River Zambesi. Though Rhodes never visited

the Victoria Falls, he wanted the bridge to be erected, in Pauling's words, 'at a spot where, when the wind is in a certain direction, it is washed by the spray from the Falls'. The tender for the bridge was won not by Pauling – 'I was sorry we had not the honour of building the bridge, but honour of that kind can be purchased at too heavy a price' – but by the Cleveland Bridge & Engineering Co. Ltd of Darlington, Co. Durham, with a bid of £72,000.

Design work was entrusted to George Andrew Hobson of London-based consultants Sir Douglas Fox & Partners, with calculations done by Ralph Freeman, who went on to design the Sydney Harbour Bridge. It is a tribute to the quality of design and planning that it took only nine weeks to erect the steelwork across the river, but before that could begin it was necessary to create a means of transporting plant across the gorge.

This was achieved in late 1903 by establishing an overhead carrier with a capacity of 10–12 tons, nicknamed 'Blondin' after the famous French tightrope walker Charles Blondin who had crossed the Niagara Falls in 1859. A rocket attached to a fine string was fired across the chasm, which enabled a cord to be pulled across and then a wire and finally a thick steel cable. This allowed one person at a time to cross the river in a bosun's chair while an even stronger steel rope was hauled across for the electrically driven winch. A few brave tourists availed themselves of the opportunity to cross the gorge at 10 shillings a head. Electricity was generated on the south bank by a portable steam engine driving a dynamo.

The Blondin not only allowed steelwork for the bridge to be carried across but also materials for the railway onward to Livingstone. This included a small steam locomotive which was dismantled at Victoria Falls and taken across piecemeal; when the 12-ton frame and

Opposite: A Beyer Garratt crosses the Victoria Falls bridge on a special charter. The principal freight traffics across the river were copper ore and ingots, timber and coal.

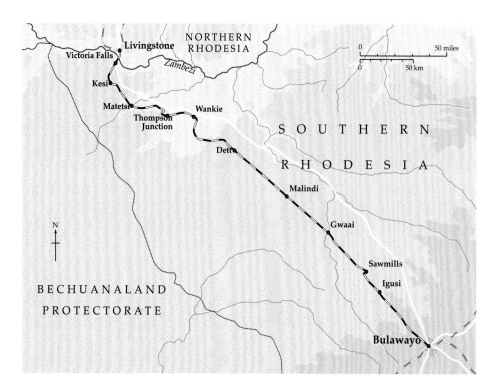

Opposite: Rhodesia Railways 15A class 4-6-4+4-6-4 Garratt No. 371 with the overnight passenger train from Victoria Falls near Mpopoma before finally arriving at Bulawayo.

cylinders were half-way across, the cable had sagged so much that the carrier stopped. Fortunately for the driver sitting in his cradle, additional current coaxed the carrier back into life and the heaviest load made it safely across. The locomotive was an 0-6-0 tank locomotive named *Jack Tar*, which had been built by Manning Wardle in Leeds in 1889 and first used to help build the Midland Railway between Dore and Chinley in the Peak District of England. Bought by Pauling & Co., it worked on the gauge widening of the Beira to Umtali railway before being employed at Victoria Falls. It can be seen today in the railway museum at Bulawayo.

The almost vertical cliff sides provided sound foundations for the concrete base in which the anchorages for the steelwork were embedded. Unfortunately, suitable foundations were not found at the expected height on the south bank, forcing the whole structure to be lowered by about 20ft (6m) and necessitating a rock cutting on the north bank. This had the unintended consequence of giving passengers the most spectacular and sudden transition onto the bridge.

The steelwork had been assembled at the Darlington works and shipped in sections to Beira in Portuguese East Africa. A young French engineer, Georges Imbault, was put in charge of construction on site, and it proceeded quickly and without serious difficulty. Imbault was supported by a team of about 30 skilled European engineers and hundreds of local African labourers, who were paid between 10 shillings and £3 a month.

By the end of March 1905 steelwork was so far advanced that the lower boom of the arch was linked. As the steelwork was erected, daily observations were taken to make sure the centre line of the bridge was being maintained, and the closing of the main arch on 1 April was a triumph: the rivet holes of the boom and cover plates aligned perfectly. A temporary track could now be laid across the open girders for lightly loaded trucks containing materials for the railway link on to Livingstone and Kalomo, which was much quicker and safer than using the Blondin.

The bridge's steelwork was treated with red lead and linseed oil before receiving three coats of Torbay

Paint of a silver-grey colour. Silver-grey was chosen not only to ensure that any patches of rust would stand out against the paintwork, but because such a light colour would reflect rather than absorb much of the sun's heat. The design also avoided the creation of any enclosed or hidden spaces within the structure where moisture could condense.

The first living creature across the bridge was apparently a fully grown leopard, possibly the same cat that was asleep on the bridge and unfortunately run over by *Jack Tar* early one morning. Imbault had promised that all traces of the construction camps would be removed and the landscape restored to its natural beauty once work was completed, so before the opening ceremony the surroundings were tidied up.

The opening of what was then the world's highest bridge took place on 12 September 1905; it was performed by Charles Darwin's son, Professor George Darwin, who happened to be in Africa leading a party of the British Association (today the British Science Association) of which he was then President. In his speech, he quoted a poetical prophecy made by his great-grandfather, Erasmus Darwin:

Soon shall thy arm unconquered steam, afar
Urge the slow barge and draw the flying car.

The locomotive on the opening train, 8th class 4-8-0 No. 54, was driven by Pauling's daughter, Blanche, and decorated with flags, palm leaves and foliage. The celebrations included a one-day regatta on the Zambesi, for which Sir Charles Metcalfe had ordered clinker-built racing fours from Oxford for the competing railway and contractors' teams as well as other crews brought up by train from South Africa. The African labourers also took part in the boat races, and a special siding was laid to take boats and spectators to the river bank. A story is told that during the day, members of the British Association party were speculating about the height of the bridge. One professor held a watch and stone in each hand, intending to time the latter's fall, but he dropped the watch instead of the stone.

Left: The Victoria Falls bridge opening party on 12 September 1905 with highly decorated 8th class 4-8-0 No.54.

Opposite: Manchester-built Beyer, Peacock 4-6-4+4-6-4 Garratt articulated locomotive crossing the Victoria Falls bridge with a special sleeping-car train in May 2015. Steam locomotives relied on the coal deposits at Wankie/Hwange which were discovered by an American in 1895.

A major alteration was made to the bridge in 1929–30 when it was decided to dispense with one of the two railway lines and widen it to accommodate a single-lane roadway and sidewalks for the many people who used the bridge to view the falls. The work was again carried out by the Cleveland Bridge & Engineering Co. Ltd; it added 13ft (4m) to the width and raised the level by 4½ft (1.4m).

The line was an immediate success thanks to the colliery at Wankie, but had its operating challenges. Between Bulawayo and Thompson Junction the land teemed with game – Wankie Game Reserve, now Hwange National Park, lies between them – and train crews waiting after dark at passing loops on the single line sometimes had anxious moments when lions roared close by. Where the line passed through the reserve, heightened telegraph poles were installed to reduce the risk of giraffes becoming entangled in them. Unfortunately elephants occasionally argued the right of way with a train, with distressing results for both. The section beyond Wankie to Victoria Falls was the bane of many an engine crew with its 1 in 50 gradients, equivalent to 1 in 37 over such curves as the notorious horseshoe bend on Katuna bank.

Within a year of opening to Livingstone, the line had dining-cars and bedding hire, and at longer wayside stops residents would often slip into the diner to have a drink and catch up with gossip.

Construction of the line on to Livingstone, Kalomo, Broken Hill and Ndola near the border with the Belgian Congo had begun before the bridge was finished, and Ndola was reached in 1909. The following year brought great excitement to the railway with the visit of a royal train in connection with the newly formed Union of South Africa. The 11 vehicles were supplemented by a cattle wagon conveying four cows to provide milk for the 12 days spent on the system. The train was based at Livingstone for four days to allow the Duke and Duchess of Connaught and Princess Patricia to visit the falls and other sites.

Many passengers came to see Victoria Falls and some stayed at the eponymous wood and iron hotel which opened in June 1904 with an Italian manager who had worked at the Savoy in London. A small launch began giving river-boat tours in 1908, or one could risk the currents in a rental canoe. Besides through trains from Bulawayo to Livingstone, a local train service linked Livingstone with Victoria Falls for the Saturday night dances at the hotel – a building which expanded and grew steadily grander. For a short time around 1916, the service was operated by a 20-seat petrol railcar ordered from the

Drewry Car Co. as agents and probably built by Baguley Cars in Burton-on-Trent. During the First World War a blockhouse was built to guard the Victoria Falls Bridge against possible sabotage from German South-West Africa.

A wide variety of steam engines worked the line, one of the most successful being the 12th class 4-8-2s built by North British in Glasgow, but the type most associated with it is the Beyer-Garratt articulated locomotive, which first entered service in 1926. Nearly half of all the locomotives made for RR were Garratts, and all but 10 were built in Manchester by Beyer, Peacock. A pair of 15th class Garratts in a handsome deep blue livery hauled the royal train to Victoria Falls in 1947.

In 1964 Northern Rhodesia became Zambia at independence. Despite the widening political differences between Zambia and Rhodesia, the former remained dependent on Bulawayo Works for heavy repairs to its steam fleet, since no workshops had been built in Northern Rhodesia. That dependence ended in 1971 with the opening of a works at Kabwe (Broken Hill).

There has been no regular passenger service across the Victoria Falls Bridge since the border between Rhodesia and Zambia was closed in February 1973. During the Rhodesia independence crisis, rail traffic was suspended, but it was restored in 1980, with goods wagons being propelled across, to be picked up by a locomotive on the other side. The bridge is occasionally crossed by Rovos Rail's luxury tourist train in its peregrinations around southern Africa. The railway in Zimbabwe deteriorated dramatically under Mugabe, and it is unlikely that a regular passenger service between Bulawayo and Livingstone will be reinstated.

BIBLIOGRAPHY

Adam-Smith, Patsy. *When We Rode the Rails*, Lansdowne, 1983.

Allen, Peter. *On the Old Lines*, Cleaver-Hume Press, 1958.

Allen, Peter and Whitehouse, P.B. *Narrow Gauge Railways of Europe*, Ian Allan, 1959.

Atthil, Robin. *The Somerset & Dorset Railway*, David & Charles, 1985.

Barrie, D.S. and Clinker, C.R. *The Somerset & Dorset Railway*, Oakwood Press, 1978.

Beebe, Lucius. *Mixed Train Daily*, Howell-North, 1961.

Beebe, Lucius and Clegg, Charles. *Virginia & Truckee*, Stanford University Press, 1955.

Berridge, P.S.A. *Couplings to the Khyber*, David & Charles, 1969.

Berry, Scyld. *Train to Julia Creek*, Hodder & Stoughton, 1985.

Biddle, Gordon. *Railways in the Landscape*, Pen & Sword, 2016.

Casserley, H.C. *Outline of Irish Railway History*, David & Charles, 1974.

Chester, Keith. *The Narrow Gauge Railways of Bosnia-Hercegovina*, Stenvalls, 2006.

Chisholm, Barbara. *Castles of the North*, Lynx Images, 2003.

Christian, Roy and Mills, Ken. *World of Southern American Steam*, Self-published, 1974.

Croxton, Anthony H. *Railways of Zimbabwe*, David & Charles, 1982.

Dangerfield, J.A. and Emerson, G.W. *Over the Garden Wall: The Story of the Otago Central Railway*, Otago Railway & Locomotive Society, 2010.

Davies, W.J.K. *The Salzkammergutlokalbahn: An Obituary*, Narrow Gauge Railway Society, undated.

Dow, Andrew. *Dow's Dictionary of Railway Quotations*, John Hopkins University Press, 2006.

Durrant, A.E. *Garratt Locomotives of the World*, David & Charles, 1981.

Durrant, A.E., Jorgensen, A.A. and Lewis, C.P. *Steam in Africa*, Hamlyn, 1981.

Fawcett, Brian. *Railways of the Andes*, Plateway Press, 1997.

Fuller, Basil. *The Ghan*, New Holland, 2009.

Garner, Adrian S. *Monorails of the 19th Century*, Lightmoor Press, 2011.

Hammond, Alan. *Life on the Somerset & Dorset Railway*, Millstream Books, 1999.

— *Spirit of the Somerset & Dorset Railway*, Millstream Books, 2003.

Haresnape, Brian. *Pullman*, Ian Allan, 1987.

Henshaw, David. *The Great Railway Conspiracy*, Leading Edge, 1991.

Hills, R.L. and Patrick, D. *Beyer, Peacock*, Venture Publications, 1998.

Holbach, Maude M. *Bosnia & Herzegovina*, John Lane, 1910.

Hoole, K. *A Regional History of the Railways of Great Britain, The North East*, David & Charles, 1974.

Hughes, Hugh. *Middle East Railways*, Continental Railway Circle, 1981.

Jennings, Paul. *Just a Few Lines*, Guinness Superlatives, 1969.

Krause, John and Grenard, Ross. *Colorado Memories of the Narrow Gauge Circle*, Carstens Publications, undated.

Leitch, D.B. *Railways of New Zealand*, David & Charles, 1972.

Marshall, John. *A Biographical Dictionary of Railway Engineers*, David & Charles, 1978.

Moir, Sydney M. *Twenty-Four Inches Apart*, Oakwood Press, 1963.

Morgan, Bryan. *The End of the Line*, Cleaver-Hulme, 1955.

Mulligan, Fergus. *One Hundred and Fifty Years of Irish Railways*, Appletree Press, 1983.

Neeleman, Gary and Neeleman, Rose. *Tracks in the Amazon*, University of Utah Press, 2014.

Nicholson, James. *The Hejaz Railway*, Stacey International, 2005.

Pauling, George. *The Chronicles of a Contractor* (ed. David Buchan), Constable, 1926.

Peacock, Bill (ed). *Main Line to Hawick*, Cheviot Publications, 1986.

Pearson, Keith. *Fell Mountain Railways*, Adam Gordon, 2011.

Pole, Graeme. *The Spiral Tunnels and the Big Hill*, Altitude Publishing, 1995.

Ransom, P.J.G. *The Mont Cenis Railway*, Twelvehead Press, 1999.

Rolt, L.T.C. and Whitehouse, P.B. *Lines of Character*, Constable, 1952.

Roth, Ralf and Polino, Marie-Noëlle. *The City and the Railway in Europe*, Ashgate, 2003.

Rowe, D. Trevor. *The Railways of South America*, Locomotives International, 2000.

Sanford, Barrie. *McCulloch's Wonder*, Whitecap Books, 2002.

— *Steel Rails & Iron Men*, Whitecap Books, 1990.

— *The pictorial history of railroading in British Columbia*, Whitecap Books, 1981.

Small, Charles. *Far Wheels*, Cleaver-Hume Press, 1959.

Smith, Martin. *British Railway Bridges & Viaducts*, Ian Allan, 1994.

Street, Jennie and Ghebreselassie, Amanuel. *Red Sea Railway*, Silver Service Consultancy, 2010.

Talbot, Frederick A. *The Railway Conquest of the World*, Heinemann, 1911.

Thomas, David St John and Whitehouse, P.B. *The Romance of Scotland's Railways*, David & Charles, 1993.

Thomas, John. *A Regional History of the Railways of Great Britain, Scotland, The Lowlands and the Borders*, David & Charles, 1993.

— *Forgotten Railways: Scotland*, David & Charles, 1981.

— *The Callander & Oban Railway*, David & Charles, 1966.

— *The North British Railway*, David & Charles, 1969.

Tourret, R. *Hedjaz Railway*, Tourret Publishing, 1989.

Turner, Robert D. *Steam on the Kettle Valley*, Sono Nis Press, 1995.

Walton, Peter. *The Stainmore & Eden Valley Railways*, Oxford Publishing Co., 1995.

Whitehouse, P. B. and Allen, Peter. *Round the World on the Narrow Gauge*, Ian Allan, 1966.

Winchester, Clarence (ed). *Railway Wonders of the World*, Waverley Book Co., undated.

Withuhn, William L. *Rails across America*, Salamander Books, 1993.

Magazines

The Engineer
The Locomotive
The Narrow Gauge
Railway Gazette International
Railway Magazine
Railway World
Today's Railways

Websites

http://www.forgottenrelics.co.uk/bridges/belah.html
http://www.irfca.org
http://www.oldmilwaukeeroad.com

INDEX

Page references in *italics* indicate images.